GOD'S
BESTSELLER

GARRY D. PIFER

Interior design: Shah Nawaz www.Fiverr.com/shah_nawaz17

Cover design: Rebecacovers

Audiobook recorded, edited, and mastered by James Ingram www.Fiverr.com/james_ingram52

Cover image: Licensed stock image, depositphotos.com

Printed in the United States of America

garrydpifer@gmail.com

DEDICATION

I dedicate this book to my best friend and amazing wife, Connie. Time and time again she has listened to my studies, read my written articles, offered her critique, and made suggestions. I believe sincerely that the Spirit spoke through her to give me direction with this book. Her encouragement along the way has been most appreciated and needed. She definitely has been an intricate part of this book. I couldn't imagine a better person to dedicate it to. Not only is she the most amazing wife, she is also a tremendous mother, grandmother and great-grandmother. She cares and loves us all so much.

Connie, I love you!

CONTENTS

FOREWORD

The Word of God promises that it can light the path of our life. This promise implies that we can improve visualization as we walk out this life by studying the words found in the Holy Bible. Specifically it says, 'Your word is a lamp to my feet And a light to my path.' Psalms 119:105 (AMP). This scripture is a hallmark to many that is usually displayed openly on items as simple as a bookmark, serving as a reminder to honor the Word of God. At times, it is displayed prominently in houses of worship or homes in general to remind all who enter of the promise. This passage of scripture has been a staple in my life, not because I find it worthy of being displayed on the wall of my living room, but because I have chosen to write it upon my heart. A lit path is more valuable to me than simply being given light to see some steps ahead. The Lord doesn't provide for us in a partial sense. He provides beyond what we could request or dream of. Usually, when this scripture is read, we think of a dark path and a lamplight or torchlight being provided. I believe that if we are students of the Word of the Lord, we will find that the Creator of the Universe will light our path of life to the point that we walk in daylight. I choose to believe that my engagement with Him and His Word can provide lighting that brings me out of darkness and into a light worthy of marvel.

1

In order to walk in the light, it is important to understand how to rightly interpret the Word of the Lord. The Apostle Paul instructed, 'Study and do your best to present yourself to God approved, a workman [tested by trial] who has no reason to be ashamed, accurately handling and skillfully teaching the word of truth.' 2 Timothy 2:15 (AMP). This mandate has become a life verse for those of us who instruct others by presenting the Word of God as The Way of Life. As a ministry founder in rural Kentucky, I find it vital that our understanding of what we read in the Holy Bible goes beyond our own life experiences or limited comprehension of it's vast meaning. It is easy to get caught up in applying what we read in the Bible to our current surroundings, dispensation of time, and especially, our Western mindset. To study is a diligent endeavor that requires devotion, application, and a willingness to have one's perspective expanded.

When I met Garry Pifer, I found him to be an astute man with a deep desire to understand the ways of God. Garry is a student by definition, his desire is to see a topic explored fully and from all angles to find the truth of the matter. Garry joined a gathering that my ministry, Uncorked, LLC, hosted that was humbly called, Morning Discussion. The premise of the gathering is to open up a topic that the group who gathers will unpack, and discern the truths about the topic found in the Word of God. Garry Pifer was born for this exercise. He began to bring articles that he would write and ask that I review and critique them. I have not found a more devoted individual to document their study than Garry

Pifer. His willingness to have his work reviewed and even challenged is confirmation of the maturity that he walks in. He began a blog that is chock full of wonderful insight into scripture, teachings of religious institutions, and current events. These articles that I am referring to captured the essence of what I believe is true study. It was evident that he would contemplate the topic for some time, gleaning a scripture here or a commentary there before he would compile his thoughts.

I was never given an article from Garry that wasn't well researched and filled with interesting tidbits that caused me to expand my thinking. I began giving Garry assignments to research for the ministry that would be included in the discussions. His writings and research have inspired many of the components of Uncorked's outreach through didactic teaching, blog writings, and instructional manuals.

"God's Bestseller: Make It Real In Your Life." is a practical guide to engaging with the Word of God. This is more than a "how to" guide to studying The Word, this is an experiential journey providing a hands on approach to becoming a detective of it. This guidebook goes beyond the principles of studying, into ways to interact with The Word of God that will captivate your life with an invitation to have your path lit. Most of us would prefer an enlightened life that provides farther sight, a safer journey, and excitement. This book provides the wisdom to truly discover The Word of God in a way that is real and produces a lasting impact on your life. I hope that you enjoy this work as much as I did. I pray that it engages your desire to pursue more of the Spirit of Wisdom that is found in cherishing the Holy Bible.

Beth Cooper, Founder

Uncorked Ministries, LLC

These were more noble than

those in Thessalonica, in that

they received the word with all

readiness of mind, and searched

the scriptures daily, whether those

things were so.

(Acts 17:11)

INTRODUCTION

I was born to parents who had no formal religious background. Both were from large families in rural America. From records that my parents kept I discovered that approximately two years before I was born my father had a desire to begin reading the Bible and my mother ordered him one from one of the mail order companies. Without a lifetime spent attending church and hearing the traditional teachings he began to see some things in his reading that didn't seem to agree with what he had heard and what those around him appeared to believe on many topics. He began listening to many of the "radio evangelists" and a few years after my birth he became part of a church organization headquartered on the West Coast.

There was no congregation to fellowship with locally. By the early 1950's my parents and I would travel several hundred miles once a year to attend a festival or convention for about a week. So, I heard the Bible read at home, heard the radio broadcasts my father was listening to and heard the sermons and messages at the annual meetings. So, I was exposed to the Bible but just like being exposed to the mumps and not getting the mumps, I didn't "get" the Bible reading and studying.

It wasn't until after high school graduation and beginning to attend the college sponsored and supported by this church organization that I began my "study" of the Bible. I was told that I should be "studying" the Bible for one-half hour or more a day. But, I don't recall anyone instructing me or my fellow students how to do that. I did find recently in some paperwork from college a three page outline entitled "How to Study the Bible Properly." I don't recall ever having seen it before, although most likely I had seen it but it apparently never made much impact. And, in reviewing it I don't find just a great lot that is really that helpful.

For the next thirty years or more I was much like most Christians. I read my Bible, generally a bit most days. A few years after graduation and moving to my home area I was made an unpaid elder in this organization and began speaking in church services and giving Bible studies. Studying and researching the Scriptures was very limited. Often it was a matter of taking what a "leading" minister in the organization had written, outlining the article and then presenting it. I suspect that many ministers have been guilty of doing a similar thing.

However, after the death of the founder of this organization in the late eighties the new leaders began introducing some new teachings and changing many long held doctrines. Consequently by the mid nineties there was a lot of confusion and consternation among the membership. Quite a number accepted the changes while a number of the ordained ministry left the organization to form and organize new churches. Of course, many of the membership followed them.

I was not readily accepting most of the changes and did join with one of the new organizations for a time. But, the greatest thing that happened to me was that I was given a desire to look into and study the Scriptures as I had never done before. I am convinced that this was from God and His Holy Spirit.

When I began on this journey I did not know the things I am presenting to you in this book. I had no training and instruction on how to study, how to search the Scriptures. I wasn't aware of any source that I could turn to for instruction and guidance. I have to give thanks to The Father and His Spirit for leading me. The things I've learned and am sharing in this book will make your searching and studying of the Bible much easier and more productive. The things I learned didn't come to me all at one time. There was a process of trial and error. You are being given the benefit of those months and years of my learning. You will be able to avoid many of the mistakes that I made. What the Holy Spirit gave me and taught me over a period of time He can lead you to understand through the following pages within the next several hours or days.

Within the pages of this book I have used some of my own Biblical studies to illustrate how to search the Scriptures. Some of my conclusions may not be in agreement with your personal beliefs or of your religious affiliation. Much of what we may find from "digging into" the Word will possibly be a bit different from what we have "heard" or been taught, but, we need to keep an open mind.

Garry D. Pifer

CHAPTER ONE

"AND SEARCHED THE SCRIPTURES DAILY, WHETHER THOSE THINGS WERE SO"

In the 1990s the church I had been a part of for decades began teaching "new doctrines" and changing long held ones. I find now in looking back that many of those changes were good, but at the time my mind was closed to them. I'm convinced that God had something else in mind for me. I don't know that I grasped until much later just what He was doing. But, I had a deep desire for the first time in my life to really look into the teachings I had received, to look at them critically from the Bible. And, as I began doing various studies I organized what I was finding and wrote my studies into essay or article form. I realized that with that organization of my thoughts I was able to put them onto paper in an understandable way.

Much later I received a revelation and understanding of Paul's words in Philippians 2:13, "For it is God which worketh in you both to will and to do of his good pleasure." It was God who put within me that desire (the will) to deeply study and gave me the natural abilities and talents to write them (to do). It was His good pleasure for me. Through the Holy Spirit, He began to reveal things that led me into truth. To begin with, most of what I studied were doctrines and teaching of the church I had been a part of. He began to show me that there was error or limited understanding in many of those teachings. In many of my studies I was led into much deeper understanding of the doctrine or teaching. To begin with I didn't always arrive at the correct conclusion because I had often worked from a wrong premise or made wrong assumptions. But, as I continued I learned through His revelation and direction how to avoid many of those mistakes.

Also, as He began to show me so much more from His Word in recent years I had to scrap many of the essays/studies that I had done and/or heavily edit them. I had put many onto a website for a period of time and then later onto a blog. As I began to see error or lack of proper understanding in a number of those items I had written, I blocked all access to my blog. Later, I started over with new and rewritten articles.

Some time after beginning my studies and writing I began to identify with the statement regarding the Jewish people Paul was speaking to in Berea, recorded for us in Acts 17:11. It says of these people, "These were more noble than those in Thessalonica, in that they received the word with all readiness of mind, and searched the scriptures daily, whether those things were so." It seemed that God was telling me that His desire for me was to look into the various doctrines, teachings, and questions that were presented by not only the church I had been a part of but most of Christianity and religion, to determine if "those things were so."

Many of my studies led me to arrive at biblically based conclusions that differed greatly from what was generally taught and believed, by the church I had been a part of as well as by much of Christianity. I have heard many others state that when they receive revelation and understanding they desire to share it with others. And, that has been my desire as well. But, sadly, I have found that many, if not most of those, that I attempt to share with are not like the Berean's who received with "readiness of mind." In fact many wish to argue or empathically reject whatever I might present to them. Sadly, most haven't been open to study it for themselves.

I feel that God gave me a special desire to search and study the Word and to understand what it really tells us. He wants, not just me, but each of us to study, to examine, to prove all things He has given us in His Holy Word. In this chapter I want us to look at some of the verses that instructs us to be doing so. And, then as we continue in this book, we will look at quite a number of things together and you can hopefully catch the vision of how you too can dig into and search for truth.

A few years ago I came across a quotation that I think would be appropriate to insert here before we begin. Theologian J. I. Packer writes this:[1]

We do not start our Christian lives by working out our faith for ourselves; it is mediated to us by Christian tradition, in the form of sermons, books and established patterns of church life and fellowship. We read our Bibles in the light of what we have learned from these sources; we approach Scripture with minds already formed by the mass of accepted opinions and viewpoints with which we have come into contact, in both the Church and the world. It is easy to be unaware that it has happened; it is hard to begin to realize how profoundly tradition in this sense has moulded us. But we are forbidden to become enslaved to human tradition, either secular or Christian, whether it be "catholic" tradition, or "critical" tradition, or "ecumenical" tradition. We may never assume the complete rightness of our own established ways of thought and practice and excuse ourselves the duty of testing and reforming them by Scriptures.

Dr. Packer's comment is exactly what we will be pursuing in this chapter, and throughout the book, learning to test and reform many of our beliefs, by the inspired Word. Let us begin. A number of bible study aids will be mentioned as we get into this chapter. We will discuss the use of these aids in Chapter Four. As our title is taken from Acts 17:11 let us start there.

Let us get the setting here in chapter 17. Verse 1 tells us that Paul and his associates had been in Thessalonica. The following verses outline the difficulties they had faced there. In verse 10 we find that Paul and Silas were sent out by night and came to the city of Berea. Once there, Paul went first into the local synagogue and spoke the gospel message to the Jews. Now let us read verse 11. "These [these particular Jews] were more noble [or generous minded] than those in Thessalonica [where they had just come from]." In what way, we might ask? "In that they received the word with all readiness of mind," with eagerness and with an open mind. "And searched the scriptures daily, whether those things were so." It becomes clear from what Luke is recording for us, that these individuals didn't just take and accept what Paul was stating and explaining to them, but they went directly to the Scriptures, the Old Testament, to check out his words. Did the Word really say what he was saying it did? I believe this passage is recorded here for us to take to heart. We also need to be "more noble" and receive what we are taught with a "readiness of mind," with an eagerness, but also with a desire to double check, to search out what the Word truly says.

Just as Dr. Packer stated, we most often take what we have read or heard or have learned over the years and let that shape what we believe. Most of us have attended church our whole life but, we need to ask, "Have I ever done just as the individuals at

Berea were doing?" Each of us needs to search the Scriptures daily, not just one time, but on a continuous basis. That requires effort. That requires digging into the Word. That requires study.

Let us look at another passage penned by the apostle Paul, 1 Thessalonians 5:21, "Prove all things; hold fast that which is good." The word translated "prove" is from the Greek word *dokimazo,* Strong's number G1381. The basic meaning is "to test." It is translated as "allow, discern, examine, like, approve, try." This verse follows upon the heels of verse 20 in which he tells us to "despise not propheseyings." In other words, take what is spoken or we hear and examine it, prove it. Then, notice the last part of verse 21, "hold fast that which is good." Once we have searched it out, examined it, proved it, then we can accept it and hang onto it. We need never be shaken on that particular point or issue again.

Notice a couple of other translations of this verse. From the Message Bible, "Check out everything, and keep only what's good." The New Living Translations says, "But test everything that is said, hold onto what is good."

I draw our attention to an Old Testament passage, Isaiah 8:20. This was being spoken to those under the old covenant but can be equally applied to the new covenant Scriptures. "To the law and to the testimony [let us apply this to the New Testament Scriptures]; if they speak not according to this word, it is because there is no light in them." How are we to know if what is being spoken is according to the Word or not? The only way is to be reading and studying the Word. We need to be searching, examining, proving that what is being said is truly what the Word says. And, if it doesn't, it is clear that those speaking have no light in them. In that case we don't hold fast but we reject it and dig deeper to see what it does say.

A verse that most of us have heard and quite likely have committed to memory is 2 Timothy 3:16; "All scripture is given by inspiration of God, and is profitable for doctrine, for reproof, for correction, for instruction in righteousness:" This verse is jam packed with information but I'd like to draw our attention to a couple of things. Paul says that all Scripture is God- breathed and is profitable for, first, doctrine. Doctrine means "teaching and instruction." By reading and studying the Scriptures we are taught. Secondly, he says it is profitable for "reproof." Often we take that to mean the same thing as the next item he mentions, correction. However, the Greek word *elegchos*, Strong's number G1650, means "a proof, that by which a thing is proved or tested." We prove or test what is told us by going into the Scriptures and searching to see what the Word says. We are able to "prove all things" by testing and examining what the Scripture actually says and comparing it to what we may have been told and taught.

Most of us are familiar with the Scripture that says, "grow in grace and knowledge." That is a bit of variation of what is recorded in 2 Peter 3:18. Some time ago I looked at that verse in context of the whole book of Second Peter. Peter uses two different Greek words in the book which have been translated "knowledge" in English. I won't give you the whole study but we find that Peter speaks about "knowledge" in verses 2 and 3 of the first chapter. Here the Greek word that is translated "knowledge" is *epignosis* (number G1922 in Strong's). It is a noun that is defined in the lexicon as "precise and correct knowledge." *Vine's Expository Dictionary of Biblical Words* gives us a bit more information. He says, "denotes 'exact or full knowledge, discernment, recognition,'" Also, "expressing a fuller or full 'knowledge,' a greater participation by the 'knower' in the object 'known,' thus more powerfully influencing him." It is not found in the Gospels or Acts. Paul uses it fifteen times (sixteen if Hebrews 10:26 is included) out of the twenty occurrences; Peter four times, all in his second epistle."

More information can be discovered when we look at the verb form of the word in Strong's and in Vines. In summary of all of the definitions we find that in almost all of the places it is used it is speaking of our "knowledge" of God and Jesus. A special "full knowledge, discernment, recognitions." It has to do with our "participation" in and relationship with God.

As we keep reading in this first chapter of 2 Peter we find in verses 5, 6 and 7 that Peter begins to give us some specific instructions. Notice, "And beside this, giving all diligence, add to your faith virtue; and to virtue knowledge; And to knowledge temperance; and to temperance patience; and to patience godliness; And to godliness brotherly kindness; and to brotherly kindness charity." We see in verse 5 that to the "knowledge," the relationship we have with God and Jesus, and to the great promises we have been given, we are to ADD something. We are told to add to our faith virtue and then comes KNOWLEDGE. I found that the word "knowledge" as used in verses 5 and 6 is translated from a different Greek word. It is *gnosis,* number G1108 in Strong's. It is defined as "knowledge signifies in general intelligence, understanding." Vine's adds, "primarily 'a seeking to know, an inquiry, investigation,' denotes in the NT, 'knowledge,' especially of spiritual truth."

When we look at 2 Peter 3:18 we find that the word "knowledge" is from the Greek *gnosis.* Reviewing the definition we just looked at this tells us that we need to increase in our knowledge and understanding of spiritual truth, that we need to be studying and searching to know and understand what is true, growing in both grace and in knowledge.

Solomon, the wisest man who ever lived gave us much of his wisdom in the book of Proverbs. Over and over again he tells us that we need to get knowledge and understanding, that we should "cry after knowledge," to "seek it as silver." In Proverbs 2:6 he says "For the Lord giveth wisdom: out of his mouth cometh knowledge and understanding." In verse 10 we are told that "...and knowledge is pleasant unto thy soul." The Hebrew word Solomon uses throughout the book of Proverbs is *da'ath,* Strong's number H1847. It is defined by Brown-Driver-Briggs' Hebrew Definitions as "knowledge, perception, skill, discernment, understanding, wisdom." I believe we often feel that Solomon is speaking only of general knowledge of the world around us, science, etc. And, it probably does pertain to that in many areas but primarily it is speaking about knowing of and about God.

A very powerful verse to me is Proverbs 25:2, "It is the glory of God to conceal a thing: but the honour of kings is to search out a matter." I especially like the Passion Translation's rendering of this, "God conceals the revelation of His word in the hiding place of his glory. But the honor of kings is revealed by how they thoroughly search out the deeper meaning of all that God says." I don't believe it is incorrect to view this in line with what John recorded for us in Revelation 1:5 and 6 and also chapter 5 and verse 10 "And from Jesus Christ, who is the faithful witness, and the first begotten of the dead, and the prince of the kings of the earth. Unto him that loved us, and washed us from our sins in his own blood, and hath made us kings and priests unto God and his Father; to him be glory and dominion for ever and ever. Amen." "And hast made us unto our God kings and priests: and we shall reign on the earth." It is an honor for us as kings to search out the deeper meaning and the truth of all that God says, to grow in knowledge and understanding.

The Hebrew word translated "glory" in the statement that "it is the glory of God to conceal a thing" is *ka'bo'd*, Strong's number H3519. Among the definitions is "splendor or copiousness" and is translated "glorious, gloriously, glory, honour, honourable."

Did you catch that? It is also translated as "honour" and that is exactly what we find in the last portion of Proverbs 25:2, "but the honour of kings." Just as it is glory of God to conceal a thing it is also glory or honour for kings, us, you and me, to search out a matter. How great is that? And, if one checks various other translations you will find that many do translate it "glory" in both places in this verse.

We are all aware that Jesus spoke in parables often. The parable of the "sower" is recorded for us in Matthew 13, Mark 4, and Luke 8. We'll look at Matthew 13. In verse 2 we find that He is speaking to the multitudes. Afterwards the disciples asked Him why He spoke in parables, verse 10. He answered in verse 11 that it was given to them, His disciples (that includes us as followers of Jesus) to know the mysteries of the kingdom, that it was not given to them, the multitudes. He explained that the eyes of the multitudes were blinded, that they seeing still couldn't see or hearing they couldn't understand. In verse 16 He tells us that "But blessed are your eyes, for they see: and your ears, for they hear." Yes, we can understand the words of Scripture, unto us has been given to understand mysteries. Yet we must be searching.

As we begin to wrap up this chapter let us look at a few verses from Jesus' "Sermon on the Mount." In Matthew chapter 7 we see in verse 1 His statement about not judging. Then let us begin reading with verse 3. Here He teaches about the mote in our brother's eye and the beam that is in ours. There are many lessons that the Messiah is teaching but I want us to specifically notice that removing the beam from our own eye is so that "then shalt thou see clearly." Yes, I know it continues on to say that we may be able to cast the mote out of our brother's eye. But, there is more here for us. In verse 6 He gives us instruction about caring for what is holy, the Word. We are told to not give it to the dogs or swine. God's Word, the Scriptures are to be respected and handled with care.

Now we come to the verses I specifically wanted us to look at, verses 7 and 8. Jesus tells us to **ask**, to **seek**, and to **knock.** (emphasis mine) What does He want us asking for? We need to see whatever it is, hence the instruction to get the beam out of our eyes so we can see clearly. As will be pointed out over and over again in this book our primary beginning point needs to be that of asking a question or questions. And, it is very important then to be asking for revelation and for the leading of the Holy Spirit. Notice that Jesus states that when we ask it shall be given to us.

After telling us to ask He tells us to seek. Just what does that mean? Notice some of the definitions given by Strong's and Thayer's lexicons, "endeavor, inquire, to seek by thinking, meditating, reasoning, to inquire into, strive after." Over in John 16:19 this Greek word is translated "inquire." Jesus, speaking to His disciples asked, "Do ye inquire among yourselves of that I said" Inquiring into something is seeking. When our inquiry is into the Scriptures we are seeking understanding of what has

21

been hidden and buried for us to uncover. Seeking and asking seem to go hand-in-hand. However, seeking goes beyond mere asking. This is a pursuit, not only of Jesus, but knowledge, wisdom and truth.

The third thing Jesus tells us to do is to knock. One person made the statement that knocking assumes a certain curiosity. I would agree. When we think of knocking we generally think of knocking at someone's door. In John 10:9 we read that Jesus states that He is the door. I believe if one "knocks" on that door in humility and with a hunger to know and understand the Word and the Truth, the door shall open. What all is opened when we knock? Luke 24:45 says that Jesus "opened he their understanding, that they might understand the scriptures." The Scriptures are closed and "locked" until they are opened to us by the Holy Spirit. Anyone can read the Bible but God's wisdom and knowledge comes by Spiritual discernment (1 Cor. 2:14).

Hopefully each and every one of us will grasp the challenge and the injunction given throughout the Scriptures to search, to seek, to dig into the words of the Bible with the leading of the Holy Spirit. We each need to get excited about what God has for us when we begin this exercise.

In the next chapter we'll begin to explore the how-to's of searching and studying the Word.

CHAPTER TWO

A PRACTICAL EXAMPLE OF HOW TO STUDY THE BIBLE

In this chapter we want to begin looking at some of the ways we approach studying and searching the Scriptures. This little study is one I did by looking at a single phrase within a verse. As you read through this study, make yourself some notes as to the various things one can do and in what order one may wish to do them. After you have read through this study we will rehearse what you have jotted down.

Many years ago when I entered college, one supported by the church I was a part of, I was told that I needed to be reading and studying the Bible at least a half hour a day. However, I can't remember ever being instructed in how to study. I believe that many Christians are in the same place, knowing they need to read and study God's Word, but just not sure how to go about it.

We live in an unprecedented time when it comes to being able to study the Bible. Remembering back all those years ago, I had one Bible, a King James Version. I had no other aids whatsoever. I did acquire a Bible dictionary and a *Cruden's Concordance* within a few months. I never had a *Strong's Concordance*, until I "married" one. My new wife brought along the one she had obtained. If I wished to check anything further I would need to go to the library, and even though it was the library of a college that stressed and taught the Bible, it was still inadequate. Today most of us have more helps on our phones and tablets than the library had. We have the internet, and almost any kind of aid we might wish is at our fingertips. But, do we know how to use these or how to go about doing a study?

Recently at our weekly get-together a verse was referred to and a brief statement made. The verse was Acts 18:21. The King James Version renders it this way "But [Paul] bade them farewell, saying, I must by all means keep this feast that cometh in Jerusalem: but I will return unto you, if God will. And he sailed from Ephesus." Here Paul was addressing the church at Ephesus. The comment at our gathering, was made, that Paul wanted to get to Jerusalem to celebrate the upcoming feast. Up until recent months I would have made the same comment. As a matter of fact, this verse was a "proof text" in the church I was a part of that was quoted showing that Paul kept the feast days and that we should also be keeping them.

Over the last few years I had been brought to understand so much concerning the new covenant, Paul's words regarding not being under the Law, the Law being death, and life was through Christ. I came to see, as he explained in Colossians 2:16–17, the sacrifices, the holy days, new moons, and sabbaths were all shadows but that *now* we have the body, the one who had been casting the shadow, Jesus. All these things were no longer needed. We needn't remain in the shadows as we are now in the Light, Jesus.

A year or so ago, as I was reading through the book of Acts and came to this verse I did something that we all should be doing, and something I never did much of in the past. That was to keep my mind in gear and ask questions. I know that many, if not most, of us read the Bible regularly. For many years I read from a Bible reading plan that took me completely through the Bible in a year's time. I am not putting that down, but one can become so focused on ticking off the boxes, in seeing that we read the designated chapters each day, that we never really pay attention to what we are reading and seldom ask any questions.

So as I read this verse, I asked, "Just what is this?" Paul teaches throughout the book of Acts and the many letters he wrote to the churches about not being under the law. Is he really saying he needed to get to Jerusalem so he can celebrate this feast? It is obvious that he isn't following the Torah command to go up to Jerusalem three times a year. Many years go by in which he never makes the journey to Jerusalem. So, step 1, I asked the question, "What is this?" Step 2, where do I go next?

My method is to check other Bible versions to see how other translators may have rendered the passage. I have e-Sword on my computer and am able to compare the verse I'm studying in all the Bible translations I have downloaded into the program.

At the time of this writing there are sixteen different versions. As I compared I discovered something very interesting. Only six versions contained this phrase, "I must by all means keep this feast that cometh in Jerusalem." And one of those has those words in italics. So, what have we here?

What is step 3? Again, this is my approach. I look at Bible commentaries. Keep in mind that these are just that, comments, made by men. But, they can be very helpful when it comes to historical background, information regarding the various manuscripts used in the translations, and so on. As I began this step, I found that many, not all, but many, of the commentators indicated that there might be a situation here. They stated that many of the manuscripts used did not contain this phrase at all. Notice just a couple of the comments. From Adam Clarke [2]"The whole of this clause, I must by all means keep this feast that cometh in Jerusalem, is wanting in ABE, six others; with the Coptic, Ethiopic, Armenian, and Vulgate."[3] John Gill says, "the Vulgate Latin and Ethiopic versions omit this clause."[4] Robertson's *Word Pictures* says, "The Textus Receptus has here a sentence not in the best MSS."

I mentioned earlier about checking various translations, which I did on e-Sword. Just out of curiosity I went onto the internet and pulled up a couple of listings of parallel versions. I ended up finding approximately seventy versions, many of which were unfamiliar to me. Of those, slightly over one half did not have this clause.

Now, is this clause truly in the original or not? Based on what evidence we have it appears that it doesn't line up with all of the rest of Paul's teaching. However, let us continue our study.

Most of you have heard the comment that to understand a passage one needs to look at the context. In this little study this would be step 4. Let us back up to verse 1 of the chapter. We see that Paul came to Corinth. You can read through all of this but we find in verse 11 he spent a year and six months here. Then, we are told in verse 18, that after this he tarried, or stayed there, a good while and then left, sailing into Syria. Verse 19 says he came to Ephesus. Verse 20 says that the people of Ephesus desired him to stay longer but he didn't agree to this. For now let us read verse 21 without the clause in question, "But bade them farewell, saying, but I will return again unto you, if God will. And he sailed from Ephesus." Continuing with verse 22 we are told he "landed at Caesarea" and after "saluting" the church he went down to Antioch. Then, verse 23 says he left there after some time and went over the country of Galatia and Phrygia.

Verses 24 through 28 tells us about Apollos and how Aquilla and Pricilla gave him additional teaching. Afterwards he went to Achaia and exhorted the disciples there.

Now, returning to the account of Paul, notice chapter 19 and verse 1, "And it came to pass, that, while Apollos was at Corinth, Paul having passed through the upper coasts came to Ephesus:" This appears to be what he had promised them in verse 21 of chapter 18. Now notice verse 8 "And he went into the synagogue, and spake boldly for the space of three months." Then in verses 9 and 10 we find that he was "disputing daily in the school of one Tyrannus," which "continued by the space of two years". We see no indications of any effort being made to get to Jerusalem.

But, what if this clause *is* in the original? How would we understand it? Is there anything else we can look at?

Step 5 for me would be to look at some word definitions. In the phrase we are questioning a key word to check would be the word "keep." When we read this word in our English Bible we interpret it to mean "celebrate." Could it have any other meaning from the original Greek?

Once again we can go to our Bible programs or to the internet and check both *Strong's Concordance* and *Thayer's Greek Definitions*. The Greek word that is translated as "keep" in Acts 18:21 is Strong's number G4160, *poieo*. Strong's says that this word occurs 576 times in the King James Version. The King James Concordance says 596 times. Both Strong's and Thayer's gives a long list of definitions. The King James Concordance lists the various ways this Greek word is translated. In those 596 occurrences the word is translated 76 different ways. Maybe, then, "keep" isn't just what Paul would have indicated? Out of the 596 occurrences *poieo* is translated "keep" only two, that's *two*, times. It is translated "keepeth" and "kept" one time each.

Both Strong's and Thayer's gives the primary definition as "to make." One word that they both gave as a meaning was "spend," or "with designation of time: to pass, spend." Is this possibly what Paul was saying, "I must by all means *spend* this feast that cometh in Jerusalem?" Some of the commentaries suggest that Paul may have wished to be in attendance for the purpose of seeing many of his friends and countrymen, and having the most favorable opportunity to preach the Gospel to thousands who would attend at Jerusalem on that occasion.

As we can see from this little example of how to study a passage or subject there may not be a clear cut answer. That is where we rely upon the Holy Spirit to lead us into truth.

Okay, from your notes, what was the approach to studying this phrase in this verse? Did you notice that the very first item was to ask a question? Remembering that in chapter 1 we looked at Jesus' words in the Sermon on the Mount; ask, seek, and knock. As we read we need to keep our minds engaged and ask ourselves questions. Just as I questioned why Paul would make such a statement of keeping an old covenant feast, that was the starting point of my search.

What was the next step in our little example? Yes, checking other Bible translations. That won't often be as clear-cut as in this instance, but will often give clarity because all translators don't choose the same English word to express the Greek or Hebrew word. Just because a translator uses a different word than what others have used doesn't make it correct, but it does lead us to deeper levels in our search.

In cases similar to this one, checking with various Bible commentators can be helpful. I again issue caution in relying too heavily on commentators. They are men with their own opinions. Unless the comment is giving us historical details or information regarding the manuscripts we need to consider what they say in light of the clear teaching of the Scriptures. Unfortunately, some will latch on to what a commentator says because it bolsters the opinion they already hold. We need to be extremely careful to not do this if we are truly seeking to understand and uncover the truth. Although it has not been emphasized, it is vital that in beginning any study we lay aside our own preconceived ideas and beliefs. Let us prove all things from the Word.

The context of a phrase, verse or passage is always to be noted. Keep in mind that the verse, paragraph, and chapter breaks were not in the original writings. They have all been added, so don't just stop reading at the end of a verse or especially the end of the chapter. In our study we continued on from Acts 18 into chapter 19 to get the whole story.

Word meanings can greatly affect our understanding. If we are reading from the King James Version or another older version many of the English words are archaic and the meaning may have changed since 1611. As mentioned above, a translator may select a different word to reflect what he believes the meaning to be. Looking at the various ways a Greek or Hebrew word can be accurately translated can be very revealing. Although the English word may be an accurate translation it may not be the meaning the writer intended. We may have to be a bit of a detective to read the context and determine what valid word fits in that place.

I hope this little exercise gives you an idea of how you can search the Scriptures. We'll go a bit deeper in the next chapter.

CHAPTER THREE

STUDYING A VERSE OR A WORD

In this chapter we will look at another study that I did a few months ago. Once again I would ask that you make notes as you read through as to the approach to doing our search. I believe you should find most of the same steps we used in the example in chapter 2. After you have read through this study we will once again recap the steps that were taken and help you cement in your minds how you would do an independent study.

"...the Times of This Ignorance God Winked At"

While in the midst of another study, Acts 17:30 came to mind. So I turned to it and read , "And the times of this ignorance God winked at; but now commandeth all men everywhere to repent." What was Paul saying? What did he mean that God winked at "this ignorance"? My questions were the first step of another study.

As I usually do when beginning to study a Scripture or passage I checked various translations. This is step 2. A few translations follow what the King James Version has, "winked," but most I found used the word "overlooked." This was more clear, but I still was uncertain just what was meant by this.

As I have mentioned in other studies, commentaries are just various men's comments, but they can sometimes give some insight. So, step 3, I checked a number of commentaries. Most seemed to feel that the times of this ignorance was prior to the gospel message of Jesus Christ. [5]John Gill's explanation really didn't appear to agree with what I am seeing of the God of the Bible. Just so that I don't misquote him by trying to paraphrase what he said, I'll quote him verbatim. "but rather the sense is, he despised this, and them for it, and was displeased and angry with them; and as an evidence of such contempt and indignation, he overlooked them, and took no notice of them, and gave them no revelation to direct them, nor prophets to instruct them and left them to their stupidity and ignorance."[5] No, I don't agree that is at all what is being said here.

To help us come to understand, let us look at the context and not just at this one verse. We can look at the whole story, but let us pick it up in verse 15. We find that Paul is brought to Athens. While he waited for Silas and Timothy to join him (verse 16) he was stirred in his spirit seeing that the whole city was given to idolatry. Verse 17 tells us that he "disputed" with the Jews and other religious people in the synagogue and in the market. In verse 18 we are told that certain philosophers encountered him. They had apparently heard him speak and some referred to him as a "babbler," and some said he seemed to be one who was setting forth strange gods. So, in verse 19 we find that they took him up to Mars' Hill and asked him to share more of "this new doctrine." In a parenthetical clause we are told that these individuals spent their time in doing nothing else but to tell or listen to someone else giving some new thing.

Then beginning in verse 22 we are told of Paul's message. He begins by addressing them as the men of Athens and tells them that he has perceived that they were in all things too superstitious, or perhaps better rendered, more religious than others. He tells them (verse 23) that he had seen all of their "devotions" or idols and sacred items. He states that he had seen an altar with the inscription "TO THE UNKNOWN GOD." We will come back to this but I feel that we find a key to understanding verse 30, when Paul speaks of this altar with it's inscription and says "Whom therefore ye ignorantly worship, him declare I unto you."

Then verse 24 through verse 29 Paul declares the *true* God to these Athenians. Paul declares Him as the Creator, the giver of life and breath, one that can not be contained in any man made building. It is good to read these verses in their entirety but I won't go through them all here. But let us read verse 29 and also verse 30 again. "Forasmuch then as we are the offspring of God, we ought not to think that the Godhead is like unto gold, or silver, or stone, graven by art and man's device. And the times of this ignorance God winked at; but now commandeth all men everywhere to repent."

So, what do we find here? Paul concludes his message of revelation of who this unknown God is by stating clearly that He is so much more than gold or silver or stone. And then he states "And the times of this ignorance." What ignorance is he referring to? Let us return to verse 23 that I said we would come back to. Notice again what Paul says in reference to this altar with the inscription, "Whom therefore ye **ignorantly** worship." "This ignorance" in verse 30 undoubtedly is their ignorance of the True God. So, Paul states that "the times of this ignorance," all the preceding time up to that moment of revelation through his message to them, God winked at or overlooked., He wasn't declaring them guilty of idolatry. However, Paul continues, **"now** commandeth all men everywhere to repent." Repentance is to change one's mind, to change the way of thinking and that cannot be done until revelation and understanding comes. It is **"now"** when ignorance is no longer an excuse that one must repent, change the mind and way of thinking.

Jesus gave us the same basic teaching. In Luke 12, verses 47 and 48 we read the conclusion of a teaching He was giving. "And that servant, which knew his lord's will [wasn't ignorant of what his lord expected and had given him to do], and prepared not himself, neither did according to his will, shall be beaten with many stripes. But he that knew not [was ignorant], and did commit things worthy of stripes, shall be beaten with few stripes. For unto whosoever much is given, of him shall be much required: and to whom men have committed much, of him they will ask the more." The one in ignorance is not held to the same accountability as the one who knows.

James tells us, James 4:17, "Therefore to him that knoweth to do good, and doeth it not, to him it is sin." While in ignorance, not knowing to do good, sin was not imputed. However, once the knowledge to do good came he was "commanded to repent," to change his thinking and his ways. If not, then it was sin.

Paul tells us in Romans 5:13 that even prior to the giving of the old covenant there was sin in the world; however since His law was not codified and written down, that sin was not imputed or charged to the individuals account. But once the covenant was made and He had given His laws, written them on tablets of stone, the people were no longer in ignorance. When they sinned, transgressed those laws, He declared them guilty, and that sin was imputed and put to their account.

By God's wonderful grace we have our sins and unrighteousness "winked at" while in our ignorance. But, when revelation comes, then He commands us to repent, change our thinking and actions. John tells us in Revelation 12:9 that the devil, the adversary, has deceived the whole world. That includes you and me. We may not all be in the same deception. You may have received revelation that I have not yet received. I may have been given insight and revelation in areas that you are still in deception about, are still in blindness. God is "winking" or overlooking my ignorance and your ignorance. However, once revelation comes He commands us to repent, to change our way of thinking.

It has been my experience that when the Spirit leads us into truth, when we are given revelation, we can become very judgmental of others who may still be in their ignorance. We may begin to compare ourselves among ourselves, which Paul tells us is unwise, and somehow begin to feel that we are somehow superior to or in some way better than others. Paul tells us in Romans 14 that we should not be judging another if they believe and do things differently. He says, "Who art thou that judgest another man's servant?" Our view of others should be just as God's view. We need to "wink at" and overlook any ignorance that may be there and concentrate on truly repenting and changing our own thinking. Of course, we may be praying for others to receive the revelation we have received but must keep in mind that it is in His "due season" and leave it in His hands.

After reading this study and watching for some of the steps we discussed in the last chapter, what did you clearly see? Right at the very beginning, in the very first paragraph, I'm sure most of you saw, step 1, a question being asked "What did he mean?" This set the stage for our searching, our seeking, to understand what was recorded for us.

Paragraph two moved us right into the next logical step, step 2, as previously pointed out, of checking other translations of the Bible. This revealed a word that was used more frequently than the word in question, "winked." However, if you were on your toes you probably noticed something missing that which would have been a help at this stage of our study. There was no move to check the lexicons to see what they reveal as to the usage of the word and other definitions. Had that been done something of interest would have been discovered. The word translated "winked" is used here in this verse and nowhere else in the New Testament. We are unable to compare the translation in other biblical passages. We would have discovered the word "overlooked" was the definition given by both *Strong's* and *Thayer's*.

Context is the next step, our usual step 4, used in this study and we find that in the fourth paragraph. By looking back, at least to verse 15, we are able to pull together the usage by Paul of the words "ignorance" and "ignorantly." Most likely you picked up on the fact that more questions were raised, more "asking" was being done. The question was asked, "What ignorance is he referring to?" By asking additional questions as we proceed in our study we are able to narrow our focus to arrive at what the context is truly telling us.

Several paragraphs are spent in looking at other scriptural passages which support the answer we are arriving at from this whole passage in Acts 17. Paul told us in 2 Corinthians 13:1 that "In the mouth of two or three witnesses shall every word be established." Whatever we are studying, it helps establish any conclusion we are beginning to come to if we find corroborating Scriptures. A single passage or Scripture without further support as to it's meaning leaves us with more searching to do.

I have referred to such Bible study helps as *Strong's* and *Thayer's*. In the next chapter I want to discuss with you many of the readily available aids and how you can use them. If you have never used a concordance or a commentary you might be a bit intimidated but you have nothing to fear. These aids are simple to use but will make your studying and search of the Scriptures much more effective.

Then in chapter 5 we will do another exercise, but we will be looking at a verse that is used to support a popular doctrine, not just an unclear phrase or word. The approach to studying will be shown to be the same. The major challenge will be one we may run into frequently in our pursuit of truth and understanding, and that is stripping away our long- held beliefs and teaching and approach the study with an open and ready mind.

CHAPTER FOUR

USING BIBLE AIDS TO FACILITATE YOUR SEARCH

I have mentioned various Bible aids in the previous chapters but I feel that we need to take this chapter to look at some of the aids most of us have readily available and discuss briefly how to use them. Just using the basics of these aids will make our search much easier and faster. As was mentioned earlier, most of us have internet access and numerous programs on our phones and computers (or can install them there) so we don't always have to pull big, thick books from the shelf.

The most important aid that we all have available to us is the Holy Spirit. On the night Jesus was betrayed He told His disciples that He would be sending the Comforter, the Holy Spirit. In John 16:13 He stated "Howbeit when he, the Spirit of truth, is come, he will guide you into all truth:" The word translated "guide" in this verse is translated "lead" in other places. As a guide or one who leads, the Holy Spirit is there to aid us in our studying and searching of the Word.

One of the verses in which the Greek is translated "lead" is in Luke 6:39. Jesus is speaking a parable and He asked, "Can the blind lead the blind?" Just as a sighted person leads a blind individual, the Spirit leads us. I once drew an analogy of a sighted person leading a blind person into a shopping mall and guiding him to the various stores within the mall. However, I envisioned this mall to be the "Truth Mall." Each of us, as the spiritually blind, will be led into this mall and to the "stores" of the Truth we are pursuing. We aren't all led to the exact same "stores," particularly if we are led into the mall through different entrances. As we looked at the study on "winked," we noted that each of us is in ignorance in some ways, but of different things. The Spirit leads us to the "stores" we need to obtain the particular truth we are searching for at that time.

We can not over emphasize the importance of praying for the leading and guiding of the Spirit. Then we can turn to using the many other aids that are available to us.

Perhaps the most used aid for most students of the Bible is the *Exhaustive Concordance of the Bible* by James Strong. This work, which was accomplished after thirty-five years of effort by Mr. Strong and his staff, was first published in 1890. Often we refer to it as "Strong's." And just what is it? The original title as given in my 1963 edition is quite descriptive: "The Exhaustive Concordance of the Bible: Showing Every Word of the Text of the Common English Version of the Canonical Books, and Every Occurrence of Each Word in Regular Order: Together with A Comparative Concordance of the Authorized and Revised Versions, Including the American Variations; Also Brief Dictionaries of the Hebrew and Greek Words of the Original, with References to the English Words." Quite a title!

So, just exactly how do we use such a book? The primary use by most of us is as a concordance. This means that if we perhaps recall some of the wording of a passage we would like to find, but have no idea where it is, we can look up that word and be directed to every place in the King James Version where that word occurs. For example let us look up the word "search." We will find a listing of every Scripture in order from Genesis to Revelation. Before we get to the listing we will be given related words we can look up. In this case we find "searched; searchest; searcheth; searching; unsearchable." In the listing of locations for the word "search" we are given the passage location, the first one being "Le 27:33" (Leviticus). Following this is a short portion quoted from this verse. Then on the right of this we will find a number. This is perhaps the most popular use for most of us as this is an assigned number for the Hebrew in the Old Testament or Greek in the New Testament. This is part of the lexicon function of the book.

Following the concordance section of the volume is this lexicon function. In my copy it is listed as "Dictionary of The Hebrew Bible" and an additional section as "A Concise Dictionary of the words in The Greek Testament With Their Renderings in the Authorized English Version." Let us continue with our example. The first listing for "search" in the concordance gave us the number 1239. All of the numbers assigned to the Hebrew words are listed in numerical order in "The Hebrew Dictionary." When we look up 1239 we find a great deal of information. First we are given the Hebrew word in Hebrew followed by the English transliteration. A pronunciation guide is given. Then we get to the dictionary function. In our example we are told that this word is "a prim. root; prop." Additional information on its derivation is given and then various definitions with a listing of the ways in which this word is translated in various places.

You may be thinking to yourself, "This is a lot of work to check all of this." And, yes, when one has to use the book it is a bit of labor. But, thankfully we live in the computer age and all of this information is at our fingertips, whether on our computer, phone, or internet. Most of the information is given to us in one listing, with the exception of the complete listing of all the places the word is used. However, most Bible programs (and most are free) also perform this function for you with just a few keystrokes. I use e-Sword but there are many other good ones available. If you don't have such a program I would suggest that obtaining one would be a high priority in your journey of searching the word.

I will mention another concordance that you might want to become familiar with. Since getting the Bible program on my computer I seldom use this book; however you might find a need or desire for it. *Young's Analytical Concordance to the Bible* has been cross-referenced to the Strong's Greek and Hebrew numbering system. The uniqueness of this book is that it lists each word in English by the Hebrew or Greek word. The downside, for me at least, is that one has to turn to the back of the book and look up the Hebrew or Greek word to obtain the Strong's number and how it is translated.

Another lexicon we mentioned earlier is *Thayer's Greek-English Lexicon*. It was prepared by Joseph Henry Thayer and introduced in 1889 after about three decades of work. This is the publisher's description: "For over a century, Thayer's has been lauded as one of the best New Testament lexicons available for any student of New Testament Greek. This lexicon provides dictionary definitions for each word and relates each word to its New Testament usage and categorizes its nuances of meaning. It also offers exhaustive coverage of New Testament Greek words, as well as extensive quotation of extra-biblical word usage and background sources consulted and quoted. This lexicon is coded to Strong's for those with little or no Greek knowledge." Since the definitions are sometimes a bit more extensive than Strong's I like to consult both. Again, both are available in most Bible programs for computers.

Brown-Driver-Briggs Hebrew and English Lexicon (or BDB) is a very helpful aid for checking Hebrew and Aramaic definitions. Most modern editions have added the Strong's numbers. This is another aid that has been around for some time, first published in 1906. Once again, this lexicon is included with most Bible programs for computers.

Another Bible aid that I use regularly and would recommend is *Vine's Expository Dictionary of Biblical Words*. It is the combined effort of W. E. Vine, Merrill F. Unger and William White Jr. Although the Old Testament with Hebrew words is not as complete as the New Testament Greek it is a very good resource. It also is listed with Strong's numbering, gives the Greek word in Greek (or Hebrew word in Hebrew) and generally a little more extensive definition. Often various passages are referred to in giving the usage of the word.

I mentioned previously that one of the first Bible aids that I obtained was a Bible dictionary. This book is as labeled, a dictionary of things biblical. There are many available. The one I first obtained was the [6]*Davis Dictionary of the Bible.* The preface explains their goal for their dictionary: "The book aims to be a dictionary of the Bible, not of speculation about the Bible. It seeks to furnish a thorough acquaintance with things biblical. To this end it has been made a compendium of the facts stated in the Scriptures, and of explanatory and supplementary material drawn from the records of the ancient peoples contemporary with Israel."[6] Bible dictionaries are most helpful with giving information about individuals, peoples, nations, countries, and so on that we find mentioned in the Scriptures.

I have mentioned commentaries a couple of times. I have never felt the need to purchase a commentary. Most are multivolume works costing a lot of money. Most Bible programs offer several at no cost and most can be accessed on the internet. I again repeat the caution given in earlier chapters. Commentaries are comments by men, many who have studied the Bible, ancient languages, etc. But, they, like the rest of us have beliefs founded on their teachings. They may or may not be correct with what they give us. The historical information and insight into the Greek and Hebrew manuscripts is in most cases of benefit.

There are quite a number of Bible commentaries available either on the internet or on the Bible programs you may have on your computer. I'll give you a bit of information on just a few of the ones I most often use, and which were offered at no cost on e-Sword that I use.

Adam Clarke was a British Methodist theologian who is chiefly remembered for writing a commentary of the Bible, a project that took him forty years to complete. It was originally published in eight volumes beginning in 1810 and continuing through 1826.

Albert Barne's *Notes on the Bible* was also published in the 1800's. It was reported that more than one million volumes had been distributed by 1870.

John Gill, an English Baptist pastor, published his Exposition of The Whole Bible in increments. First were the three volumes on the New Testament that were published from 1746–48. This was followed up with the six volumes covering the Old Testament, 1748–63. It is available in one package on most of our Bible programs.

The *Jamieson, Fausset and Brown Bible Commentary* authored by Robert Jamieson, Andrew Robert Fausset, and David Brown was first published in 1871. It is most often referred to as the JFB Commentary.

Matthew Henry produced his *Exposition of the Old and New Testaments* from 1708–10. Actually he had only finished the portions on the Old Testament, the Gospels and the book of Acts before his death. The balance was finished by thirteen others.

Archibald Thomas Robertson authored *Robertson's Word Pictures in the New Testament*. It was produced in six volumes from 1930–33. Information on his work states that he focuses on key words and explains various shades of meaning that are implicit in the Greek text but often lost in translation.

These commentaries are ones that I am personally familiar with but you may wish to check out some of the newer commentaries. *The Moody Bible Commentary* is a good work in one volume. John MacArthur has a multivolume commentary on the New Testament.

There are many additional Bible aids available. Many are designed for the "professional theologian" or student of Hebrew and Greek. That leaves out most of us. The aids discussed will get you a good ways down the road in your pursuit of understanding of the Scriptures. Just a final word, don't assume that since you can look up the Hebrew and/or Greek word in the concordance that you are now a Greek or Hebrew scholar. As the old saying goes, "A little knowledge is a dangerous thing."

Before we conclude this chapter, I need to clarify a bit what I alluded to earlier about the Bible study programs that we are able to put onto our computers and other devices. Searching for a word doesn't entail the laborious task associated with using a book. Most have a search feature that works similar to the internet search engines, except that generally only a word or two is going to work. If we put in one or two words, we will get a listing of every place those words are used. You are able to narrow your search somewhat by specifying what Bible translation you are searching, if more than one word you can ask that verses with all the words or verses with any of the words be obtained and if you want the search to be of the entire Bible or a designated portion. In addition to searching by a word or words a very helpful feature is doing a search by the Strong's number. Sometimes the English word may be translated from a number of Greek or Hebrew words. We can then search by the number for the word used in a particular passage and find all of the places that the Greek or Hebrew word occurred.

What facilitates my searches for the Greek and Hebrew words is having the King James Version of the Bible with the

Strong's numbers. I can simply "click" on the number and having selected Strong's or Thayer's or another resource I can obtain all the information for that particular number.

With my program I was able to obtain the King James Commentary. Now this is a bit different from the other commentaries we have mentioned. For example, if one has checked Strong's for a particular Greek or Hebrew word, as just mentioned above, I can then select this commentary, designated as KJC in my program. It gives me the word in Hebrew or Greek, the English transliteration, the total number of occurrences in the KJV and then each English word that it has been translated as, with a Scripture listing of each place it is used.

As I recounted earlier, when I first began to read and study the Bible various aids were not readily available and accessible. As Scripture states, to whom much is given much is required (Luke 12:45). We have been given much in the way of aids, mostly free and readily at hand. Let us make good use of them.

Before we move on to the next chapter I'd like to make mention of something that you may have wondered about. We have referenced Greek, Hebrew, and Aramaic. These are the main languages the Bible was originally written in. The Old Testament was primarily written in the Hebrew language. In about the third and second centuries B.C. the Hebrew Bible was translated into Greek, commonly known as the Septuagint. The New Testament was mostly written in Greek and Aramaic. All of these Scriptures were translated into Latin and the common language

Bibles, such as our English language Bible, were translated from those Latin translations. Very few of our aids reference the Latin, instead mostly, the Greek and Hebrew.

CHAPTER FIVE

STUDYING A VERSE THAT SUPPORTS A POPULAR TEACHING

A s I mentioned at the end of chapter 3, we will be doing an exercise in this chapter which entails doing a study of a verse that is used frequently to support a popular teaching. I know that this may be a teaching or at least something that you have been told repeatedly. Anytime we begin to ask questions about something that we believe and have been taught it is difficult to open-mindedly do such a study. If, however, we are truly committed to searching out the Word to see "whether those things were so" we must learn to set aside our beliefs, our preconceived ideas, our established ways of thought. I know that it is hard. However, if we are truly sincere in our desire to search out the hidden things of God we must do so. Seek the Holy Spirit's assistance. We need not do this on our own.

The study we will be looking at here is of John 14:2. I hear this verse referred to very often with the absolute statement of what this is supposedly saying. I asked, the first step in our process of searching, is what is being stated "so?" As you read through this study make a note as to what is the approach, what was done. I want you to note down anything you see that may be different or an addition to what we have covered in the previous exercises.

"In my Father's house are many mansions"

John 14:2, "In my Father's house are many mansions: if it were not so, I would have told you. I go to prepare a place for you." This verse is quoted or referred to frequently by Christian ministers, who believe that Jesus was telling His followers that He was going to be going to heaven shortly and that He was going to be preparing a big and beautiful home, or mansion for them. It is taught that at the end of life one's spirit would immediately go to heaven and would reside in one of these mansions.

Is this what Jesus was teaching here in John 14? Is that the context of this passage? Is the Father's house heaven? What was Jesus teaching His disciples in this passage of Scripture?

Let us first look at the context of Jesus' statement. After having washed the apostles feet Jesus sat down and began to speak to them. Then after Judas left Jesus began in greater detail to instruct them. In verses 33 and 36 of chapter 13 He told them that where He was going they could not come, that they could not follow Him. Then in chapter 14 Jesus begins instructing them about the Holy Spirit and the ministry of the Holy Spirit. This instruction continues on through chapters 14, 15, 16, and 17.

52

So, how does verse 2 of chapter 14 fit into this teaching? I believe we need to answer a few simple and basic questions in order to understand.

When Jesus speaks of "the Father's house" is He speaking of heaven? That is the common assumption and teaching. The expression "father's house" is used throughout the Old Testament in referring to the family, the household, a family of descendants. In the New Testament the expression is only used four times and two times it is used exactly as it was used in the Old Testament. But, we do find Jesus using this expression twice, both in the book of John. One time is here in John 14:2. The other is found in John 2:16: "And said unto them that sold doves, Take these things hence; make not my Father's house an house of merchandise." He was here referring to the temple.

I believe it should be mentioned that although the temple was referred to by Jesus as "His Father's house" and was called in the Old Testament the House of God and the House of the Lord, it was acknowledged that God did not reside in a building made with hands. First Kings 8:27 explains, "But will God indeed dwell on the earth? behold, the heaven and heaven of heavens cannot contain thee; how much less this house that I have builded?" Acts 7:47–49, in his message, Stephen says, "But Solomon built him a house. Howbeit the most High dwelleth not in temples made with hands; as saith the prophet, Heaven is my throne, and earth is my footstool: what house will ye build me? saith the Lord: or what is the place of my rest?" And Acts 17:24:

"God that made the world and all things therein, seeing that he is Lord of heaven and earth, dwelleth not in temples made with hands"

Although the temple was called the House of the Lord or the House of God throughout the Old Testament, that was a shortened statement of a house that was built for the name of the Lord God of Israel, (see 1 Kings 8:17,20). Notice what David said in reference to the temple in 1 Chronicles 28:2: "Then David the king stood up upon his feet, and said, Hear me, my brethren, and my people: As for me, I had in mine heart to build an house of rest for the ark of the covenant of the LORD, and for the footstool of our God, and had made ready for the building."

Let us return to John 2. Immediately following His statement we read in verse 16, Jesus made an interesting statement to the Jews who were seeking a sign from Him. Verse 19, tells us, "Jesus answered and said unto them, Destroy this temple, and in three days I will raise it up." They, of course, thought He was speaking of the temple that He had just cast the money changers out of, but, notice what He was speaking of! Verse 21:"But He spake of the temple of His body."

Maybe when we read John 14:2 in context, we will begin to see what Jesus was speaking about when He said "In my Father's house." The physical building of the temple was not where the Father was dwelling. Where was He dwelling? Jesus proceeded to tell His apostles and us where the Father was dwelling. All of the verses, 3 on down are important, but let us draw our attention to verses 10 and 11 "Believest thou not that I am in the Father, and the Father **in me?** the words that I speak unto you I speak not of myself: **but the Father that dwelleth in me,** He doeth the works. Believe me that I am in the Father, and **the Father in me: He doeth the works."** (emphasis mine) Let us go back to verse 2. "In my Father's house," is *not* speaking of heaven. Jesus is telling His apostles and us that He was the Father's house, where the Father was dwelling. He was the only one on earth at that time that the Father was dwelling in. That was to change and that is what Jesus is proceeding to tell them and us. Let us continue reading "In my Father's house are many mansions." Okay, what is He saying? Not that "mansions" is a wrong translation, but it meant something different in 1611 than it does now. And, it is a word that in the Greek is only used two times in the entire New Testament (we will look at the other instance momentarily) and is translated differently and more clearly in the second occurrence.

Look at what *Vine's Expository Dictionary of Biblical Words* has to say (Strong's number G3438) *mone* "Primarily 'a staying, abiding (akin to *meno*, 'to abide'), denotes an 'abode'" Thayers's concordance defines *mone* "1.) A staying, abiding, dwelling, abode 2.) To make an (ones) abode 3.) Metaphorically of the God the Holy Spirit indwelling believers."

Let us read verse 2 with understanding: "In my Father's house are many abiding places, many places of abode, many dwelling places." Are we beginning to see what Jesus is saying?

Earlier He had told them that He would build His church. Paul in his writings really clarifies the fact that we abide in Jesus' body, the church. In His body, the church, there is plenty of room for all of us to dwell.

Notice the last part of verse 2: "I go to prepare a place for you." He isn't speaking of building them and us fancy homes in heaven. He was preparing for us to dwell in Him, in His body, the church. Only after His death and resurrection could we enter into His body and dwell there. As we continue to read Jesus' teaching in chapter 14 He speaks of sending the Holy Spirit to indwell us. Verse 20 clearly tells us that we are to be in Him, Jesus "At that day ye shall know that I am in my Father, and **ye in me**, and I in you." (emphasis mine)

Let us look at verse 23 and perhaps we will see something that we may never have seen before. "Jesus answered and said unto him, If a man love me, he will keep my words: and my Father will love him, and we [Jesus and the Father] will come unto him, and make our mansion with him." Wait a minute! It says "our abode" with him. If you will check the concordance the word translated "abode" here is the same word, and the second place it is used, that is rendered "mansions" in verse 2.

Jesus was *not* teaching that He was going to heaven to prepare some big, fancy houses for us, but was teaching that after His death and resurrection the Holy Spirit was to come into His apostles and all born again believers. And, through that Spirit He and the Father would make their abode, their home, with us.

Paul speaks of the mystery, which is Christ in us. And, not only Christ, but He says here that the Father will dwell and make His abode with us as well. No longer would Jesus be the only one that the Father was dwelling in, the only one that was "the Father's house," *but* we now are the Father's house, the house of God. Notice a couple of Scriptures. First Timothy 3:15: "But if I tarry long, that thou mayest know how thou oughtest to behave thyself in **the house of God, which is the church** of the living God, the pillar and ground of the truth"(emphasis mine). First Peter 4:17: "For the time is come that judgment must begin at the **house of God**: and **if it first begin at us**, what shall the end be of them that obey not the gospel of God?" (emphasis mine)

When we let the Bible interpret itself, rather than accept what religion tells us, we can understand some powerful truths. The truth that we, the church, are now the house, the dwelling place of God the Father, Jesus Christ and the Holy Spirit is awesome!

Okay. The study was begun by stating the verse in question and mentioning how it is often used or mentioned. The question for the study to center on was our wondering "whether these things were so." After "asking," the next step taken was to look at the context. Although we don't spend the time to look at the following chapters, it is mentioned that these are a part of the context. Following reading and looking at the context more questions are put forth. This helps us pinpoint specifically what we are wanting to answer by our study. A study can try to cover too much territory and get into other rabbit trails which would be better left for another time.

Although not stated, most will realize that other aids were used to determine the usage of the expression "father's house." By using Strong's we must do a bit of digging because we have two words to look at and then try to find them used together. One of the features that most of the Bible programs, such as e-Sword that I use has, is a search feature where one can search for Scriptures that would have the two words in them, not necessarily together. That narrows the time and effort down in locating Scriptures that do have the two words right together. This is just another tip we hadn't previously given.

After looking at the various passages that had these two words together, we could soon determine that the similar usage was in John 2. We once again have a look at context. When we return to John 14:2, we do the word study. There is no fixed order in which the various steps are taken, but it seems to be a logical progression. Although no direct statement is made I believe you realized that to find the Greek word and the meaning we would have gone to Strong's, Thayer's, or Vine's. Following the word study for "mansions" in verse 2 we proceed with more context study of the rest of the fourteenth chapter. When doing our word study we would have discovered the different translation in verse 23. This would begin to bring a clearer answer to our original question.

The final step in this study was to check out the phrase "the house of God" and see some Scriptures that would support what we were discovering. The concluding statement in the study is what we want to achieve from all of our studies, to let the Bible interpret itself. We want to see clearly what the truth is that has been hidden for us, not from us. It is there for us to search out.

As we near the end of this chapter we might reflect on what we have covered so far. The simple studies to try and search out the meaning and get understanding from a verse with a key phrase or word was relatively simple. As we began to do broader searches to understand a teaching or a statement that is being made about a passage, we find that the search becomes a bit more extensive. For for the most part, we continue to use the basic things we covered in the simpler studies–ask questions, do word studies, check translations, consult commentaries. And, depending on the particular study, we don't always use each of these. Commentaries on the verse we just went through would likely repeat what is most widely proclaimed. Above all we must be like those at Berea and look at and receive the Word with "readiness of mind."

CHAPTER SIX

DOING A MAJOR TOPIC STUDY

Thus far we have looked at doing a study of a word or phrase within a verse or passage of Scripture. How do we proceed when there is a major topic we wish to search into? We will continue to use the same basic steps we have been covering, however we will have to break our study into a number of smaller studies. Just as when someone once asked, "How do you eat an elephant?" the answer was "One bite at a time," the conclusion or answer to the question from the larger study has to be added to what we discover in the subsequent small studies.

I'll walk you through a major study that I did a number of years ago. The church that I was a part of held to the doctrine, as most churches do, of tithing. The primary teaching was that the very first 10 percent of any thing I earned "belonged to the church." It was expressed that it belonged to God, but that meant it was to be given to the church. I was challenged to do a study when someone asked whether it would be proper to use that first

10 percent to help someone in need, instead of giving it to the church. That was now my question, the asking part of the study.

As I began to think about how to study this topic, I soon realized that the question of using that first 10 percent to help someone was only a tiny bit of the real question. What about tithing? Is it a universal law that has always existed? Or was there a starting point? And, if so, is it still in effect today? I began to see that these also were only a part of the major study that needed to be done in order to answer that initial question.

Just where should one begin such a major study? After doing the tithing study, I wrote my conclusions in an essay. I reasoned, "A beginning point is to define the word tithe." To do that I went to Strong's and searched for the word "tithe" and checked the definitions of the Hebrew and Greek words that had been translated as "tithe." I had a perception in my mind before hand but this short bit of checking solidified that. I knew, had heard, or read some of the "proof texts" concerning tithing. So, for me this was where I started. I searched out where these passages were in the Bible and tackled each one as a small study.

The first one I studied was the one most often quoted by Christian ministers, Malachi 3:8: "Will a man rob God? Yet ye have robbed me. But ye say, Wherein have we robbed thee? In tithes and offerings." I had been told that if I didn't pay my tithes I was robbing God. Then further, verse 9 was read or quoted, "Ye are cursed with a curse: for ye have robbed me, even the whole nation." I had to ask additional questions, my study had to go further. As we covered earlier, we need to get the context. We need to ascertain a number of things, but to begin with we need to see who is being spoken to. Is the writer of the book speaking to me and to you? My search began to expand. To answer my question, I went back to the very first verse of the book of Malachi and read it through to the end of the book. I won't spoil all of this for you. You can do that reading on your own. Once I found who was being addressed I had at least one brick to build my wall of study to answer my original question.

In the initial search for the word "tithe" in Strong's, I had discovered that the word only appears two times prior to the time of Moses and the giving of the Law. Checking out these passages seemed to be appropriate. The first place was when Abram returned from the recovery of his nephew Lot and the goods and people of the kings of Sodom and Gomorrah. We read in Genesis 14:20 that Abram gave Melchizedek "tithes of all." More questions were being brought to the study. Does this account establish that there was a law regarding tithing from the time of creation? Did Abram always tithe, or was this a one- time event? Was tithing enjoined on conquering kings to tithe ten percent of all of the spoils of war? What items were to be tithed on? Were these goods being tithed on Abram's in the first place? Oh, you can see that many more questions often need to be answered before we ever answer our initial query. To study this particular story, we need to consider the context. We need to search to determine whether spoils of war were ever included in the tithing laws we find given later. Also, we need to search those laws to see just what was to be tithed. As you can begin to see, one small question may lead to numerous studies in order to search out the answer.

I noted that there were two places that discussed or mentioned tithing before the giving of the Law, so looking at the other one after spending time on the story of Abram was in order for me. We'll look at that story in a bit more detail in the next chapter. It is the story of Jacob and his vow to tithe.

What were the laws regarding tithing? Our search for truth and understanding took us to the book of Exodus and the giving of the Law at Mount Sinai and what was recorded by Moses in the books of Exodus, Leviticus, Numbers, and Deuteronomy. Searching the book of Exodus where the Ten commandments and all of the other laws are enumerated we don't find tithing mentioned. Even though there is nothing to study there the absence of any mention is revealing in itself. Actually, we don't find any information in the book of Leviticus until we come to the last five verses of the very last chapter. Interesting. Studying the context and adding what we find to some of the things we found in our other studies, particularly the story of Jacob, sheds more light on the subject.

Also, we begin to receive an answer to the question on what is to be tithed on. Another search is necessitated to dig into this question more deeply. In the five verses of Leviticus 27, we also get some revelation to answer another of our questions: is the tithe on the first tenth? As we continue our search into the laws of tithing found in Numbers and Deuteronomy, we keep adding to our accumulation of information about tithing.

After I had looked at all of the Scriptures on the subject found in the Old Testament I wanted to see what Jesus and the writers of the New Testament had recorded for us. After all, if tithing is for you and me we should find something given to us in the New Testament writings. In checking Strong's I discovered that tithing is discussed in only eight verses in all of the New Testament—two are parallel accounts of the same teaching by Jesus, and one other passage was within a parable taught by Jesus. The remaining five are all found in the book of Hebrews. In studying all of these, context is important.

I won't go into all that I discovered in my study. However, I think you can see that such a study will take a while to accomplish. It is just a series of smaller studies. Once we complete them, it is a matter of taking all our answers we arrived at and put those altogether to arrive at the answer to our original question or questions.

This study on the subject of tithing took me several weeks. I had to lay aside some long- held teachings, much like what we covered in the last chapter. I had to be honest with what I was discovering as I did each of the smaller studies. Doing a major topic study may be a bit daunting but broken down into smaller studies it isn't so overwhelming. You may wish to begin your searching of the Scriptures with some smaller studies to feel comfortable. Or, at the beginning of a larger topic, ask numerous questions and select one of those to start with. You can and will be able to "search out a matter," as Proverbs 25:2 says. It is quite rewarding to find your answer and know you have done as 1 Thessalonians 5:21 tells us: "Prove all things."

CHAPTER SEVEN

CONTEXT—VERSE BY VERSE STUDY

I told you in the last chapter that we would look at the story of Jacob contained in the 28th chapter of Genesis. This study is a long hard look at what is given to us regarding Jacob and his dream from God, his response, and the vow he made. It is a rather lengthy article that I wrote up after doing my study, but I think it highlights what we want to cover. So I'm going to put the entire article into this chapter. I will not wait to the end to comment and point out the process of the study, but will insert the comments as we go along. I'll try to do so between paragraphs and made obvious notations that the comments are separate from the study itself.

DID JACOB TITHE?

In an essay a long-time elder in the organization that I was once a part of, says in speaking of Jacob, "His attitude was 'Of all that You will give me from this day forward, I will surely give the tenth to You.'" Did Jacob tithe from "this day forward"? The same author says, speaking of Jacob, and I quote, "But he does say, 'From now on I will tithe; I will give the tenth of all that I possess.'" Did Jacob say that? Did he tithe on all that he possessed from that day on? Let us study the account being referred to. It is recorded for us in Genesis 28.

NOTE: In this first paragraph we have laid out the questions we are asking and wish to answer as a result of our study.

Before we turn to this chapter and begin our study let us review just who Jacob was. Jacob and Esau were the twin sons of Isaac and Rebekah, the grandsons of Abraham and Sarah. Isaac was born to Abraham and Sarah when she was long past the childbearing years, a direct miracle from God. The Scriptures tell us that Abraham was one hundred years old and Sarah was ninety when Isaac was born. Isaac was forty years old when he married Rebekah. However, Rebekah was barren. Isaac entreated God on behalf of his wife and God heard his prayer. When Isaac was sixty years old, the twins were born. When Isaac was "old" (Gen. 27:1), somewhere over one hundred years old, he called Esau to himself and asked for "savoury meat" that he might eat it and then bless Esau. We are familiar with the deceit that Jacob and his mother worked to get Isaac's blessing upon Jacob.

NOTE: This paragraph is inserted here before our study of chapter 28 begins, establishing the background. Most likely if you were doing this study you might already be familiar with the story. If you begin a similar study of something to answer your own question or questions and you aren't all that familiar with the characters and or the setting, a short side study would be in order.

We now come to chapter 28 of Genesis. In the last verses of chapter 27 Rebekah tells Isaac that she is wearied because of the women Esau had married and expresses her concern that Jacob might follow suit. Isaac called Jacob to him, chapter 28:1–2, and commanded him not to take a wife from the daughters of the people of the land of Canaan. He instructed him to go to Padanaram, to the family of his grandfather, Bethuel, and to take a daughter of his uncle Laban to be his wife.

NOTE: As we have mentioned previously, the original did not have chapter breaks, so we need to pick up the story, the context, even prior to verse 1 of chapter 28.

In verses 3 and 4 of chapter 28, we read something very interesting. Isaac pronounces a blessing upon Jacob, almost word for word what had been promised and reconfirmed to Abraham and to Isaac. There is no indication that Jacob found this strange or something new. Undoubtedly he had heard this repeated over and over in the more than forty years of his life. He knew of the Lord's appearance to Abraham, the promise given to him, the covenant He made with him. Jacob knew that the Lord had also appeared to his own father, Isaac, and had reaffirmed the promises to him. He had been told repeatedly of those promises and of the covenant God and Abraham had made. In fact, he daily was reminded of this in his own flesh, because of the token of that covenant, circumcision. (Gen. 17:10–11)

NOTE: *This is very important to the story and what will be given us in this chapter. When we are studying context we need to pay special attention to everything that is being said. We find that after giving Jacob this blessing Isaac sent him on his way, verse 5.*

So the words of the promise from God rang in Jacob's ears as he left home to journey to Padanaram. In verses 6 through 9 we read a bit of a side story. Esau saw that Isaac had blessed Jacob. He saw that Isaac had sent Jacob to the land of his grandfather to get a wife, and of how his own wives taken from Canaan was a very evil thing in the eyes of Isaac. He took another wife, a daughter of Ishmael, Abraham's son. Verse 10 brings us back to the story of Jacob.

As he was on his way toward Haran, as evening came on, he came to a place that was called Luz before being renamed (Verse 19). Since the sun had set, Jacob prepared to spend the night. He gathered some stones and using them for pillows he lay down to sleep. Verse 12 tells us that as he slept he dreamed, a dream that came from God. He saw a ladder or stairway set up on earth and the top of it reached unto heaven. He saw the angels of God ascending and descending upon it. Then in verse 13 God begins to speak to him. Let's note what God says to him.

"I *am* the LORD God of Abraham thy father, and the God of Isaac: the land whereon thou liest, to thee will I give it, and to thy seed; And thy seed shall be as the dust of the earth, and thou shalt spread abroad to the west, and to the east, and to the north, and to the south: and in thee and in thy seed shall all the families of the earth be blessed. And, behold, I *am* with thee, and will keep thee in all *places* whither thou goest, and will bring thee again into this land; for I will not leave thee, until I have done that which I have spoken to thee of."

NOTE: What God spoke is very important and we will be looking at it with a critical eye. We need to be careful in our studies that we don't just read through it all quickly and miss important details that are there.

Much of what God told him had been spoken to Abraham and to Isaac. However, some was specifically directed to Jacob. The promise of the land had been central to all repetitions of the promise. The seed being as the dust of the earth, to multiply throughout the earth, was well known. The specific statement, which we have understood to be prophetic of Jesus Christ, that in his seed all the families of the earth would be blessed had been stated over and over. But, God did personalize the promises, making very detailed and specific personal promises to Jacob. He told Jacob that He would be with him wherever he went. He also promised him that He would bring him back to "this land." God promised that He would not leave Jacob until He had done what He spoke there to him.

NOTE: As we read through verses 13–15 it is easy to run all the sentences into one statement but if we are analyzing exactly what is there and concentrate on each sentence or statement we may pick up something different. Be specific in your study.

When Jacob woke up, verse 16, he deeply grasped that God was present in that place and he had not been aware of it. It shook him up, as we would say. Verse 17 says "And he was afraid." He recognized that this place was, at least to him, the very dwelling place of God and the gateway to heaven. Early in the morning, Jacob arose and took the stones he had been using as pillows and set them up as pillars. He poured oil upon them and called the place Bethel, meaning the House of God.

Then we come to verse 20. "And Jacob vowed a vow." In many articles, booklets and writings of various authors this is not noted. It is often stated that Jacob "promised." However, the original indicated the translation to be correct, Jacob vowed a vow. Let us note what *Vine's Expository Dictionary of Biblical Words* has to say.

The vow has two basic forms, the unconditional and the conditional. The unconditional is an "oath" where someone binds himself without expecting anything in return. (Psa. 116:14) The obligation is binding upon the person who has made a "vow." The word spoken has the force of an oath which generally could not be broken: (Num. 30:2) The conditional "vow" generally had a preceding clause before the oath giving the conditions which had to come to pass before the "vow" became valid: (Gen. 28:20–22).

"Vows" usually occurred in serious situations. Jacob needed the assurance of God's presence before setting out for Padan-aram (Gen. 28:20–22); Though conditional "vows" were made out of desperation, there is no question of the binding force of the "vow." First a "vow" is always made to God. Second, a "vow" is made voluntarily. It is never associated with a life of piety or given the status of religious requirement in the Old Testament. Third, a "vow'"once made must be kept. One cannot annul the "vow."

NOTE: *Notice that in the middle of a large study we come across additional questions and need to do brief small studies. We go to some of our Bible study aids and get understanding before we proceed.*

The vow that Jacob makes is a conditional vow. Notice what he says: "if." He is negotiating with God. He begins by mentioning the personal, specific promises God has made to him, not the major promises that had been repeated over and over and that were well known by all in the family. First he says, "If God will be with me, and will keep me in this way that I go, and will give me bread to eat, and raiment to put on, so that I come again to my father's house in peace." He specifically mentioned what God had promised in verse 15 above. Notice again, "I am with thee, and will keep thee in all places whither thou goest, and will bring thee again into this land; for I will not leave thee."

Continuing with the vow he is making, verse 21, Jacob says "If" you do all of this [which we just listed] "then shall the Lord be my God." He knew of God. He knew that He was the God of Abraham and Isaac. He was vowing to develop that same close, intimate relationship they had with God. He continues his vow "And this stone, which I have set for a pillar, shall be God's house."

It is interesting to note the things Jacob vows to do. He should have been desirous of developing the close personal relationship with God, whether He bestowed those promises or not. But, declaring the stone he had set up as God's house seems to be an idea that Jacob came up with on his own. We find no similar instance recorded in the Bible.

Now let us notice the last part of Jacob's vow, the last part of verse 22, "and of all that thou shalt give me I will surely give the tenth unto thee." It was very clear that in the first part of his vow he was concentrating on the very specific and personal promises God had made. Here we see Jacob directing his vow toward the first part of God's promises, verse 13, where God addresses what He will give to Jacob and to his descendants. "The land whereon thou liest, to thee will I give it, and to thy seed;"

NOTE: I think we begin to see the importance of looking deeply at what is given us. I have not seen in any commentaries and comments made by others the notation that God is giving specific promises and that Jacob is responding to each separately in his vow to God. Many of our studies won't have that much detail to be noted but we should be very deliberate in our reading and analyzing what has been recorded for us in the Scriptures.

73

Hopefully, we can see that Jacob made a conditional vow to God to do three specific things upon God's fulfillment of His promises. The first two—a personal relationship with God and declaring the stone as God's house—were directly dealing with the very personal and specific promises God made toward Jacob relative to his journey. The third thing was to "give the tenth unto thee" of "all that thou shalt give me." This clearly is in reference to the promise of the land being given to him and his descendants.

NOTE: This paragraph we have just read is very key to answering the questions we asked at the beginning, the reasons for the study. We will often find key verses or phrases within the middle of the context we are going through.

Since "the land" was central to the promise God made and to the vow Jacob was making it is very important that we understand exactly what God is promising. Let's notice what the Scriptures tell us. Genesis 12:7 says. "Unto thy seed will I give this land." Where was Abraham when God made this statement? Notice verse 5, "and into the land of Canaan they came."

Genesis 13:15 says, "For all the land which thou seest, to thee will I give it, and to thy seed for ever." What land was Abraham seeing? Verse 12 says, "Abram dwelled in the land of Canaan." Verse 17 God instructs Abraham to "Arise, walk through the land in the length of it and in the breadth of it; for I will give it unto thee."

Genesis 15:7 says, "And he said unto him, I *am* the LORD that brought thee out of Ur of the Chaldees, to give thee this land to inherit it." In verse 18 God gets very specific as to what land He is speaking of. "In the same day the LORD made a covenant with Abram, saying, Unto thy seed have I given this land, from the river of Egypt unto the great river, the Euphrates."

Genesis 17:8 makes it very clear as to what land God is promising. "And I will give unto thee, and to thy seed after thee, the land wherein thou art a stranger, all the land of Canaan, for an everlasting possession; and I will be their God."

There are additional Scriptures prior to the promise being made to Jacob and numerous ones afterward that spell out quite clearly that the "land of promise" was Canaan.

NOTE: The above paragraphs and scriptural passages are an example of another short study to give us a bit of needed information. This will need to be done often in a longer study such as this one, perhaps even sometimes to fully understand a verse or subject of a smaller study.

The Hebrew word translated "land" in all of these verses is *erets*, H0776 in Strong's. It is used in some areas to indicate the whole earth, in others a country or territory or district or region. One of the definitions is "land of Canaan, Israel." When we look at the clear Scriptures of God we should have no doubts in our minds that the promise God made to Abraham, to Isaac and to Jacob was the land of Canaan.

When God said in the dream of Jacob's "the land whereon thou liest, to thee will I give it, and to thy seed" it was very understandable to Jacob. He knew what land was being referred to. There was no confusion in his mind in that regard. In a casual reading of the verses we might think Jacob wasn't hearing some of the rest of God's promise. In Genesis 28:15, God says, "and will bring thee again into this land." Jacob responds in verse 21, "So that I come again to my father's house in peace." When we check the Hebrew we find that the word God used in verse 15 for "land" is a different word. It is *adamah*, #H127 in Strong's. Notice the definitions of this word from Brown-Driver-Briggs.

1) ground, land

1a) ground (as general, tilled, yielding sustenance)

1b) piece of ground, a specific plot of land

1c) earth substance (for building or constructing)

1d) ground as earth's visible surface

1e) land, territory, country

1f) whole inhabited earth

1g) city in Naphtali

Notice that in some usages it means a specific piece of ground and it can refer to a specific territory or country. Clearly God is referring to the very area in which Jacob was at the moment. Why then does Jacob respond by saying "to my father's house."?

NOTE: Once again a short side study is needed. This will be a common occurrence in many of your studies. Question after question will come to mind if you are truly seeking to understand what is being told you in the passages you are reading. I often feel like I'm a detective striving to follow the clues to discover the answer. It really makes studying and searching exciting. Bible reading and studying should never be boring.

The Hebrew word translated "house" is *bayith*, H1004 in Strong's. Most times it is used it is referring to a house, a dwelling or shelter. It can refer to an entire household. I'd like to have you notice the definition as given in *Vine's Expository Dictionary of Biblical Words:* "bayit (1004), 'house or building; home; household; land.'" It can refer to the "land." Vine's says later, "In a few passages bayit means 'territory' or 'country'." So Jacob wasn't "confused." He was responding to God by saying, if I might paraphrase, "So that I come again to this land, this territory, to this promised home of my father in peace."

Before we can answer the questions we asked in the very beginning of this article we need to determine when the promises of God were received and when Jacob fulfilled the vow he made to God. The vow, as we pointed out, was conditional and it was a three-part vow. We will see from the Scriptures that God did not give all the promises at one time nor did Jacob keep all of the parts of his vow at one time.

NOTE: Okay. We are in need of more information, a need for another side study. If we aren't already acquainted with the storyline of what we are studying, we will have to do some searching with the aids at our disposal to ferret out where it is recorded. In our example here we find that it is contained in the next few chapters.

Following the making of the vow to God recorded in Genesis 28 we read the story of Jacob going on to Padanaram where he worked for his uncle Laban in exchange for his wives, Leah and Rachel. We are most likely familiar with the story of the wrong woman being given to him, the numerous times Laban changed Jacob's wages, and so on. Jacob spent twenty years with Laban—fourteen serving for his wives and six for the livestock. His wages were changed ten times (Gen. 31:41). After these twenty years he began his journey back to "his father's house," to the land his family was residing in. On the way he had to cross the land his brother Esau occupied. In fear of what his brother might do to him in retaliation for his own poor treatment of Esau, he appealed to God for His help. We read his prayer in Genesis 32:9–12. He reminded God of some of the promises He had made. Following this prayer Jacob prepared great presents for Esau and sent some of his servants off to meet Esau. He then took his wives, their servants and his eleven sons and passed over the "ford Jabbok" and sent them on over the brook (Gen. 32:22–23).

Jacob was left alone. An event occurred that we may not totally understand. It says "and there wrestled a man with him until the breaking of the day" (Gen. 32:24). Jacob recognized that he was wrestling with God. He says in verse 30 of this chapter,

"I have seen God face to face." This event was Jacob's "conversion" if you will. His name was changed by God to Israel, meaning a prince of God.

Following this event we find that Jacob and Esau were successfully reunited without the dire consequences that Jacob had feared. Jacob journeyed on to Succoth, built a house and "booths" for his cattle (Gen. 33:17). Following this he "came to Shalem, a city of Shechem, which is in the land of Canaan, when he came from Padanaram" (verse 18). He bought a parcel of a field and erected an altar and called it EleloheIsrael, God the God of Israel. Chapter 34 gives us the story of his daughter Dinah and the slaying of Hamor and Shechem.

NOTE: We find here a great amount of information as to what had transpired. More details are now to be uncovered. All of your studies will add more and more details if you stick with them and soon you will have answers to your original question or questions.

Now in chapter 35 we see some very interesting details. In verse 1 God tells Jacob to go up to Bethel, to dwell there and to make an altar to God. Jacob told his entire household to put away the "strange gods" that were among them. Verse 3 confirms that God had answered part of His promise He made to Jacob, that we read in Genesis 28.

"And let us arise, and go up to Bethel; and I will make there an altar unto God, who answered me in the day of my distress, and was with me in the way which I went." Let's review again that particular promise, Genesis 28:15. "And, behold, I am with

79

thee, and will keep thee in all places whither thou goest, and will bring thee again into this land; for I will not leave thee, until I have done that which I have spoken to thee of." Jacob confirms that God has been with him and has brought him back to Canaan.

Jacob then journeyed to "Luz, which is in the land of Canaan, that is, Bethel". Remember this is where God appeared to him in a dream and made the promises to him (Gen. 28:19). Genesis 35:7 says that Jacob built an altar there and called the place Elbethel, the God of Bethel. Verses 9 to 13 tells of the event we read in chapter 32, God appearing to Jacob again as he came out of Padanaram and blessing him, of changing his name to Israel, rehearsing the first part of His promise to Jacob.

Notice verses 14–15. "And Jacob set up a pillar in the place where he talked with him, [even] a pillar of stone: and he poured a drink offering thereon, and he poured oil thereon. And Jacob called the name of the place where God spake with him, Bethel."

NOTE: We take the information we are finding and fit it into the context we are studying. We are able to begin to draw some conclusions, maybe not a complete answer yet.

I believe it is very clear that Jacob had fulfilled two parts of his three part conditional vow. God had been with him and had brought him back to the "land." He had now made the Lord his God. He had returned to Bethel, which is "house of God." He had built an altar, set up a pillar of stone and poured upon it a drink offering and oil.

What about the central part of God's promise that had been made to Abraham, repeated to Isaac and to Jacob, the promise of the "land"? Jacob was in the land now, the land of Canaan, but he had not been given the land, he had not inherited it. As we just read in Genesis 35:11–12 God had repeated that part of His promise. Notice again verse 12: "And the land which I gave Abraham and Isaac, to thee I will give it, and to thy seed after thee will I give the land." It was still future. It was still promised to be given to Jacob and his seed.

NOTE: Yet another question has to be asked and answered. An additional small study is in store.

When did God finally give Jacob and his seed "the land"? When they finally crossed over the Jordan after wandering in the wilderness for forty years. Let's notice just a few verses out of many.

Exodus 33:1 "And the LORD said unto Moses, Depart, *and* go up hence, thou and the people which thou hast brought up out of the land of Egypt, unto the land which I sware unto Abraham, to Isaac, and to Jacob, saying, Unto thy seed will I give it".

Deuteronomy 1:8 "Behold, I have set the land before you: go in and possess the land which the LORD sware unto your fathers, Abraham, Isaac, and Jacob, to give unto them and to their seed after them."

Deuteronomy 8:1 "All the commandments which I command thee this day shall ye observe to do, that ye may live, and multiply, and go in and possess the land which the LORD sware unto your fathers".

Deuteronomy 11:8 "Therefore shall ye keep all the commandments which I command you this day, that ye may be strong, and go in and possess the land, whither ye go to possess it".

Deuteronomy 11:9 "And that ye may prolong *your* days in the land, which the LORD sware unto your fathers to give unto them and to their seed, a land that floweth with milk and honey".

Deuteronomy 11:31 "For ye shall pass over Jordan to go in to possess the land which the LORD your God giveth you, and ye shall possess it, and dwell therein".

NOTE: Again, there is a bit of searching and digging using the aids at your disposal. You may have to search using different key words. In this study we might use "possess," or "land." Searching for "land" quite possibly would give you a long list to look through. The word "possess" seems to show up with more verses pertinent to our search. It again makes you into a detective.

There are many more very clear Scriptures showing that the promise God had made was not fulfilled until the Israelites crossed over the Jordan and took possession of the land of Canaan. The final and third part of Jacob's vow: "and of all that thou shalt give me I will surely give the tenth unto thee" would not have become valid and binding until this time. When we review God's instructions regarding tithing found in Leviticus 27, it is so clear. He is giving instructions regarding payment of vows in this chapter. He tells them the tenth, the tithe of the land that Jacob had vowed to give to God was "holy to the Lord" (Lev. 27:30). It is revealed in the book of Numbers that the tribe of Levi was to receive the tithe as wages for their service in the tabernacle. They were not to receive a portion of land, an inheritance, as the other tribes did.

NOTE: Yes, another side study. A search for the word "vow" would lead you to this information in Leviticus 27.

As we conclude let us review again the statements we quoted from the essay of a long-time elder and answer the questions we asked. He made a statement in speaking of Jacob "His attitude was: 'Of all that You will give me from this day forward, I will surely give the tenth to You.'" We asked, "Did Jacob tithe from 'this day forward'?" There is no statement in the Bible to tell us that he ever tithed. He did vow to God to give a tenth, to tithe of all that God would give him, the land. That land was not given until the seed of Jacob entered Canaan several hundred years later.

NOTE: As you near the completion of your study you should review your original questions and thoughts. Ask yourself if you have reviewed and searched everything that pertains to this study, to this context, these verses you have been looking at.

The author of the essay also said, speaking of Jacob, "But he does say, 'From now on I will tithe; I will give the tenth of all that I possess.'" This statement is not found in the Bible.

NOTE: This is an important key to any study that we do. Check statements made by others, be they scholars, commentators, your pastor, or others. You may find that just like the statement I quoted from the author of an essay, it isn't found in the Bible. It may be an assumption on the part of the one writing or speaking or something they believe because someone else said it. Because someone says something can be the very reason we need to search the Scriptures.

We can, with scriptural authority, answer our primary question: "Did Jacob tithe?" We have seen from the biblical account that Jacob vowed to God to give a tenth of what God was promising him and his seed, which was the land of Canaan. We have also seen that the promise was not given to Jacob during his lifetime. Hebrews 11, the faith chapter, speaking of Abraham, says in verse 9, "By faith he sojourned in the land of promise, as in a strange country, dwelling in tabernacles with Isaac and Jacob, the heirs with him of the same promise." Then in verse 13 we read,"These all died in the faith, not having received the promises." Verse 16 says that they "now desire a better country, that is, an heavenly" [one].

No, Jacob never tithed as a requirement of his vow—he could not have done so since the conditions were never met during his lifetime.

Did he give offerings to God otherwise? Very probably so, although we aren't told how or when. We aren't told if Melchizedec was still on the scene or if there was anyone else to receive offerings. From the Scriptures we see God communicating with Jacob in a dream, appearing and wrestling with him as a man. Genesis 35:1 says, "And God said unto Jacob—" indicating a personal manner of communication. No mention is made of any person serving as a go- between or spokesperson for God. And the only offering we see that Jacob made to God was a "drink offering" (Gen. 35:14). It is possible, and probable, that he may have offered burnt offerings to God. He had Abraham's example (review the story of Isaac being offered) and we know that he erected an altar in Shalem, a city of Shechem (Gen. 33:18–20). If Jacob gave to God in any other way, it isn't stated in the Bible. And, if he did, we are not told of any percentage he may have chosen to give. Whatever it might have been it was not a stipulation of his vow to God. Of a surety it would have been given cheerfully from a willing heart. After all that is what God loves (2 Cor. 9:7).

NOTE: Even if you disagree with the conclusion to my study I believe you can see how such a study is done. Step by step, verse by verse with numerous side studies, you will arrive at an answer to the question that initiated your study.

CHAPTER EIGHT

USING THE INTERNET TO AID YOUR SEARCHES

T he internet has revolutionized our world. When once we had to dig through books at the library to find bits of information we can now search millions of documents with a click of the mouse. Many of us are "addicted" to the internet with social media, email, YouTube, and other amazing means of communication. It has jokingly been said of any statement that is made that it must be true, since it was on the internet. Hopefully, we know better than that. There is a lot of garbage and nonsense on the Web but the internet is a valuable resource, if we learn to use it properly and wisely.

It is my aim in this chapter to give you tips and ideas of how the internet can be used to search the Scriptures. I'll only be scratching the surface as I am no expert on its use. I can only share what I have personally learned and experienced. Way back in the early 1990's when home computers were beginning to become popular, I couldn't imagine why I would ever want or need such a device. A friend tried showing me some of the things he could do and how there was a "worldwide web." At that time he and I were running a small sharpening business and he contracted a local web design business and we became the first sharpening business to have a home page on the web offering sharpening services. Oh, how much things have changed since then. Out of curiosity I just did a search and found pages and pages of listings for sharpening services.

In chapter 4 we looked at various Bible study aids and one we discussed was a Bible study program for our computer or other device. To obtain such a program we need access to the internet. We will be able to search out the numerous programs that are available, look at features, find those that are free and those that can be purchased. The one that you choose will be the one that your research indicates has the features that you feel will be most helpful for you. Generally the ones that must be purchased will have more capabilities available. As I have mentioned previously, I use e-Sword. The very first program I used was Online Bible and later I used the Sword Project. I was introduced to e-Sword, and it just seemed to work a bit better for me. Thankfully we are each unique and different so "one size doesn't fit all."

Once you have selected the program you will be directed through the steps of getting it downloaded onto your device. Most will have some sort of tutorial on how to navigate through all of the features. It will soon become a comfortable and useful tool. I'm not sure how other programs work, but I know that once the basic program for e-Sword was downloaded I was able to obtain numerous Bible translations, lexicons, dictionaries, and commentaries to add to it. Although I haven't taken advantage of other items such as Bible maps and even some books they are available if one is interested. They have a simple method allowing you to select, download, and install each module. I appreciate the fact that all of this is installed onto my computer and is not web based. This means that I can use the program whether I have internet access or not.

In addition to the free Bible versions, lexicons, commentaries, and other aids you are able to obtain with your program there generally are many premium ones available for purchase if you desire. However, if you feel that the premium ones might not be used or accessed all that often, the internet has most of those available to read online at no cost to you. There are a number of websites that will provide that for you. One that I go to frequently is biblegateway.com. They have many translations of the Bible in languages other than English as well as approximately sixty different English language versions. Some of these will be those you will have on the Bible study program you choose, but others will be ones that you would have to pay a premium price for.

Other sites offer lexicons and commentaries for you to access. Having to go to a website may not be as convenient as having it at your fingertips on your device but I find that it isn't all that often that I choose to go to the additional resources. Consequently it seems a small price to pay to have those items available. One website that you might wish to check out is studylight.org. Once on that site, you will find a box labeled "Bible study tools." Clicking on this box will gain you access to over a hundred commentaries, six concordances, twenty-seven dictionaries, and eight encyclopedias. Other boxes can lead you to other resources. This is just one site. You may find others that work for you.

How else can we make use of the internet? Whatever question we may have there is sure to be someone, or many some ones, that will give us an answer. Accessing the internet with our question is much like checking a commentary. If the question is related to a historical fact or something of that nature, most likely we will be able to find an answer that will agree with all of the other answers to the question. But if we ask a question relative to a word or phrase in a Scripture or one about a biblical topic, we had better be prepared to be inundated with a plethora of varied answers. Many of the answers we receive from our inquiry may be from pastors, theologians, and other Bible students, but each one has his or her own opinion. As I heard one man express it, opinions are like noses. Everyone has one and they all have a couple of holes in them.

It was mentioned earlier that if we are serious and sincere in our searching we must put our own beliefs and preconceived ideas aside. We can't look through all the responses we might get from an internet search trying to find someone who agrees with us and assume they must be correct— after all, they agree with us! I have reminded quite a few people of the fact that we are all deceived, just maybe on different things. Revelation 12:9 states that the devil "deceiveth the whole world." That doesn't leave any of us out. If we are going to make any assumptions perhaps it should be to assume that we are probably the one who doesn't understand or have the correct answer. Even if we get a majority of answers that are in agreement, we must not assume that the answer is correct. The Bible has to be the final word, where we filter all of the answers we may have received.

A few months back I did a study on what the Bible tells us about the subject of death. More to firm up the need for such a question than any other reason I did a short internet search, asking the question "What is death?" Here are some of the responses that I received, taken from my essay after the study.

Do a quick Google search on the internet and you will find scores of definitions and ideas concerning death. Some things advanced are from a secular worldview. Others are from a biblical worldview, and even those ideas are not uniform. Here is a sampling from both secular and biblical/writers/teachers. Some of these brief statements are from blogs, some from full length articles, some from dictionaries and encyclopedias.

"Death, dying, and the afterlife are all shrouded in deep mystery, cloaked in darkness and generally surrounded by fear and apprehension. The very idea of death strikes fear into many people's hearts."[7]

"Death is the cessation of the connection between our mind and our body. Most people believe that death takes place when the heart stops beating; but this does not mean that the person has died, because his subtle mind may still remain in his body."[8]

"Death, the total cessation of life processes that eventually occurs in all living organisms. The state of human death has always been obscured by mystery and superstition, and its precise definition remains controversial, differing according to culture and legal systems."[9]

"Although there is no universally accepted definition of death, a 1971 Kansas statute comes close: 'A person will be considered medically and legally dead if, in the opinion of a physician, based on ordinary standard of medical practice, there is absence of spontaneous brain function.'"[10]

"Death is inevitable to whatever is born. The Soul is free from the bondage of birth and death. It is eternal; it has no death. Anything that is born has to die, and because there is death, there will also be birth. So death is connected to birth. Wherever there is birth there is death."[11]

"According to the Bible, death is not the end of life but the separation of the soul from the body. Scripture clearly speaks of both eternal life with God in heaven and eternal separation from God in hell."[12]

"The biblical definition of death—whether physical or spiritual—is not non-existence, but separation."[13]

Numerous sites stated that physical death is the separation of body and soul.

Looking through the various answers I received to my question, it reaffirmed the need to search the Scriptures to seek the answer, rather than those who post on the internet. We won't go through that study here, but the conclusion from the study from Holy Scriptures didn't agree with any of the answers I got from my internet search.

As was observed earlier, doing an internet search is much like reading a commentary. The answers may sound good and may make some sense, but if you aren't careful, you may be led astray. The Bible has to be the final authority. Sometimes using all of our aids to Bible study will not give us a perfectly clear answer. We may have to lay our question and our research aside for the moment, seek God's inspiration, and wait. We live in a world that wants instant gratification, that doesn't want to wait for anything. Yet, Scripture tells us that many things come to us with patience.

There are times in my Bible reading I come across a passage that I just don't understand. I ask myself the questions that are generated and begin to search for the answer. Proceeding with the steps we have outlined, I check other translations, read and study the context, check the meanings of various words in the passage, and even consult a number of commentaries. Yet I don't always obtain clarity. At this point I would quite likely turn to the internet. Instead of looking at more lexicons, I would look at articles, blogs, or other pieces written on the subject. As observed in the example about death, there will very likely be a variety of thoughts and opinions. I may not read each in great detail but quickly skim through, looking for some point that might be a bit different or that stands out for me. This isn't an *aha* moment but something that leads to another question or direction in which to take my study. I have at times found in the very midst of a piece— although I may not be in total agreement with the premise or the direction the author is going— that gem of an idea or thought that may be key to the understanding I'm searching for presents itself. And on the other hand, it may lead me down a rabbit trail that doesn't produce desired results. But many times it will help unlock the door that has been closed to understanding. I just urge that we all use all caution when doing this aspect of our search.

There are other ways the internet can be a valued asset to us in our searches. I'll discuss a bit more in a following chapter. Perhaps the biggest benefit with using the internet to do research is the time factor. Pulling books off the shelf and paging through is very time consuming. If we don't have those books, a lot more time would be taken if we made trips to the library. Many of us would be tempted to just say, "Forget it!" and not continue our study. Being able to quickly check something on the web may keep our enthusiasm alive and keep us in pursuit.

CHAPTER NINE

SEEKING TO UNDERSTAND OLD TESTAMENT SHADOWS

Saul, who became the apostle Paul, went into Arabia following his "conversion" on the road to Damascus and spent three years receiving revelation from Jesus (Gal. 1:12). Paul, we know from his own testimony, knew the "Scriptures," the Old Testament backwards and forwards. But like his brethren, the Jews, he never understood that they were speaking of Jesus, the Savior. After receiving revelation he was able to read with "new glasses." And he taught from that revelation. We read that he "taught Jesus and Him crucified" from the Scriptures. He was able to give true understanding to what had been just rules, regulations, and rituals.

He saw clearly the shadows in the sacrifices, holy days, new moons, and sabbath days (Col. 2:16–17). The Jews knew of these things contained in the old covenant but never knew they were all foreshadowing Jesus of Nazareth, who was the Messiah they were expecting. Paul explained in 2 Corinthians 3 how there had been a veil upon the heart. Paul proclaimed what he had received from Jesus when he went into the synagogue in the cities he went to. He spoke of the Passover, the days of unleavened bread, the wave sheaf offering, the feast of weeks, etc. We, as Christians, are able to see Jesus in these things because of Paul's "new glasses" and because the veil is being removed, but many times we don't see as much as we might because, unlike the Jews he spoke to, we aren't that familiar with those things that were shadows.

Some time back I decided to do a study of the wave sheaf offering. If we enter the word "wave" into the search feature in our Bible study program we find verses in Exodus and Leviticus with the word but it is linked with only the word "offering" or "breast." Scanning down the listing of verses we finally see the word "sheaf" and the word "wave" together, Leviticus 23:11. This is where we would want to begin our study. Again we need to read the context. The beginning of the paragraph is in verse 9 and we find this is the LORD's instruction to Moses concerning this particular offering. Verse 15 is a new paragraph and it begins to give instructions for something else, which is tied into this offering, but we will concentrate on what is outlined in verses 9–14.

We'll walk you through this study of the wave sheaf offering but keep in mind that any other Old Testament shadow would be dealt with in the same basic manner. Search to find where the instructions were given to Moses and the Israelites and then proceed.

We haven't stressed it but have referred to the taking of notes as we study. As we read through the verses here we need to read for detail and it is good to note those details down. Especially if other questions are generated we will be reminded when we review our notes just what other things we need to do a side study on.

The LORD's specific instruction to Moses was to speak these words to the people. His instructions weren't going to be complicated. The people would be able to understand and we shouldn't have any difficulties. Beginning in verse 10 we see what He speaks to Moses. Note what He instructs was to be done and when. When? When they entered into "the land." We have covered that earlier, the promised land, the land of Canaan. Continuing with verse 10 we see the exact time was when they reaped a harvest. What the LORD was instructing them wasn't to be acted on the day He gave it. Now, notice what they were to do. "Then ye shall bring a sheaf of the firstfruits of your harvest." You might understand a "sheaf" or think you do, but a word study would be in order. Also, what does it mean "firstfruits?" Understanding all of this will be important to understand our subject. Make notes.

In verse 11 the LORD tells exactly when after entering the land and reaping the harvest this offering was to be made and how it was to be done. If we have read through many of the instructions on other offerings we know that many were of animals that were burned on an altar. This is different. How? Why was it offered? Now He gives a bit more specific information as to the timing. When was this? "The morrow after the sabbath." What sabbath? Another side study. Checking context will give us the answer. Beginning in verse 4 the "feasts of the LORD" begin to be revealed to Israel. As we read through verses 5–8 we see the instructions are for "Passover" and "the feast of unleavened bread." If you aren't familiar with these more side studying will be in order. We do find that this feast is seven days in length. In verse 3 we would have read that the sabbath was the seventh day.

Now we can begin to answer part of the question as to when the sheaf was to be waved. "On the morrow after the sabbath." If we need to check on what "morrow" is we can quickly do so, finding it just means "tomorrow" or the day following the sabbath.

We won't continue to take you through everything, but I'm sure you begin to see that one inquiry leads to another. In this study you will eventually need to learn about how the new year was determined, how they counted time, how the first month was determined and when the Passover and feast of unleavened bread was to be celebrated. One of the important items is what this sheaf was picturing, what the later fulfillment was, and what it was a shadow of.

Without going through it all—which will be a fascinating and fulfilling study if you choose to do it—I'll give you a few of the answers, and then we'll look at some of this in the New Testament. The morrow after the sabbath would be Sunday. The Passover and feast of unleavened bread were being celebrated at the time of "Holy Week." It was that Sunday morning that Jesus arose from the grave after His crucifixion and spending three days and three nights in the grave (Matt. 12:40). In 1 Corinthians 15:23 Paul states "Christ the firstfruits." Jesus Christ was that "sheaf" that was waved, or lifted up. Remember it was "to be accepted" for the people (Lev. 23:11). That morning after His resurrection one of the first ones to see Him was Mary Magdalene. Remember what He said to her in John 20:17: "Touch me not; for I am not yet ascended to my Father:" Later that day others did touch Him. Soon after speaking with Mary He was lifted up, or waved, as that offering to be accepted for us.

Maybe this isn't as fascinating to you as it is to me. But, coming to this point I still had questions. Perhaps you might have some of the same ones. With this fulfillment of that shadow why don't we find more information in the New Testament giving us revelation of all of this? Another question, another search. Actually there has been information for us but due to some translation issues it has been hidden. I'll give you a bit of what I found and you can take it further if interested. The following is taken from the study I did.

Interestingly there are at least eight verses that refer to the wave sheaf offering in the New Testament but due to some inadequate translations they have not been seen by most of us. Those eight passages contain an English phrase we are all familiar with, "first day of the week." The Greek in seven of those is *"mia ton sabbaton."* The eighth is from the Greek *"protos sabbaton."* We'll look at these expressions and the verses in which they are used.

"First day of the week" is found in the following verses: Matthew 28:1; Mark 16: 2, 9; Luke 24:1; John 20:1, 19; Acts 20:7; 1 Corinthians 16:2. One thing you will notice when you turn to these verses is that the word "day" might be printed in italics in your Bible. Most of us are aware that a word in italics has been put there by the translators when they believe this added word makes the meaning clearer although it is not written out in the Greek text. If we leave out the word "day" we have "first of the week". But sadly that is not a truly correct and honest translation.

The first Greek word in the phrase is *"mia,"* Strong's number G3391. The definition is "one, only one." Sixty-two times in the New Testament, *"mia"* is translated "one." Only eight times is it rendered "first," and seven are the above verses with the exception of Mark 16:9. (We'll look at that verse later.) The correct and honest translation would have been "one" not "first."

The Greek word *"ton"* can be translated "of the." When you see the word *"sabbaton"* you can probably correctly guess how it should have been translated. Correct, "sabbath." In the New Testament *"sabbaton"* is translated "Sabbath Day" thirty-seven times, "Sabbath" twenty-two times and "week" nine times. Eight of the nine times it is translated "week" it is in the verses we are

looking at. The ninth verse is in Luke 18:12 and several translations have translated it "Sabbath" instead of "week". (Literal
Translation of the Bible, Concordant Literal, and Modern KJV
are a few.)

So, the correct rendering of "first day of the week" should be
"one of the Sabbaths". ("*sabbaton*" in all of these eight verses is
plural). But, just what does this mean? Let me quote a few
sources that correctly understand.

(At this point in my essay I quoted from a number of sources
but let me give you one so I don't leave you hanging.)

The following is from notes by [14]E. W. Bullinger in *The Com-*
panion Bible. The first one is at John 20:1. "The first day of the
week = on the first (day) of the Sabbaths (pl.). Gr. Te mia ton sabbaton." Dropping down he continues, "Luke 24:1 has the same.
Matthew reads, 'towards dawn of the first (day) of the Sabbaths',
and Mark (16.2), 'very early on the first (day) of the Sabbaths.
The expression is not a Hebraism, and 'Sabbaths' should not be
rendered 'week', as in A.V. and R.V._A reference to Lev.23. 15–
17 shows that this 'first day' is the first of the days for reckoning
the seven Sabbaths to Pentecost_ On this day, therefore, the Lord
became the firstfruits (vv. 10, 11) of God's resurrection harvest
(1 Cor. 15.23)."[7]

As I said, there is much more, but let us recap what we covered in how we would do a study of this nature. There are all of
the other items that Paul said were shadows that will make some
great studies for all of you so inclined. We decide on what we

wish to study: perhaps a question that has come to us from our Bible reading. We start a search to see where in the Old Testament we need to go to begin our study. Word studies, contextual studies, perhaps some other translations, and maybe even a few commentaries will be necessary. Keep notes. Follow up on additional questions that are generated. And, give yourself plenty of time, as this type of study will take a while. Don't rush. Just like a real detective, keep looking for clues, check them out, ask questions. Keep in mind what we read in Proverbs 25:2, that it is "the honour [or glory] of kings [that is you and me] to search out a matter." The picture painted by the Old Covenant laws, sacrifices, offerings, and feasts truly is a beautiful masterpiece when we see it in the correct light.

Chapter Ten

Our Beliefs—From the Bible or Tradition?

B oth Matthew and Mark were inspired to record an encounter that Jesus had with some of the religious leaders of His day, the Pharisees and Scribes who came from Jerusalem. We find this in chapter 15 of Matthew and chapter 7 of Mark.

The setting was that these individuals saw Jesus' disciples eating bread, or a meal, without washing their hands. Now, this wasn't just that they hadn't washed the dirt off of their hands but they had not done so in the vigorous and prescribed way that these individuals taught and followed. They explicitly stated that the disciples were not "holding the tradition of the elders" (Mark 7:3). Matthew 15:2 states that they asked why the disciples of Jesus "transgress the tradition of the elders" (verse 2).

Notice that Jesus, as He often did, responded first by asking these religious leaders a question rather than giving them a direct answer. Matthew 15:3 tells us, "But he answered and said unto them, Why do ye also transgress the commandment of God by your tradition?" He then cites the commandment to honor one's parents and how they, by following their tradition, were disregarding this command. He states,"Thus have ye made the commandment of God of none effect by your tradition" (verse 6). Then in verse 9, He adds, "But in vain they do worship me, teaching for doctrines the commandments of men." In Mark's account it is recorded that He mentioned a number of other things they were holding to because of their traditions (see Mark 7:7–8).

In both accounts when the Pharisees and Scribes brought their question to Jesus they stated that His disciples were not "holding the tradition of the elders." This phrase, "tradition of the elders," refers to the various rules and regulations that they had added to the Law of Moses. Rabbi Michael L. Rodkinson, who did one of the first translations of the Babylonia Talmud into English and author of the two volume *The History of the Talmud* [15]states: "The Talmud is, then, the written form of that which in the time of Jesus, was called the tradition of the elders, and to which he made frequent allusions". Note it is often called the "Oral Torah." This is not the place nor do we have the time to go into this, but when a thorough study is done it will be discovered that they were stating these rules were given to Moses and passed down orally. This is not true.

When Jesus walked the earth He adhered to the Law of Moses, as He stated in Matthew 5:17 "I am not come to destroy, but to fulfil". He, as God in the flesh, not born of Adam but of God, was able to keep the Law as no one else had ever been able to do. However, He made it plain that all the additions, all the "traditions" that had been added were of men, not of God. He did not follow or obey those traditions.

As new covenant Christians we do not focus on the Law nor are we for the most part knowledgeable of these "traditions of the elders" that the Jewish rabbis had added on to the Mosaic Law. However, have we ever thought what Jesus might say to our religious leaders of the Christian church if He were walking on the earth today? Would He possibly tell them (and us) that we are "Making the word of God of none effect through our tradition"? Just how much of what is taught and believed by many Christians is directly from the Bible and how much is "tradition"? Many have never even considered that question. We have accepted and based our belief system on what we have heard and been taught.

A few years ago I came across an interesting book written to expose the origins of many of our modern church practices, *Pagan Christianity* by Frank Viola. I'm not attempting to endorse the book but did want to share a few quotations from the introduction of the book. I believe these are good for us to consider. "As Christians, we are taught by our leaders to believe certain ideas and behave certain ways. We have a Bible, yes. But we are conditioned to read it with the lens handed to us by the Christian tradition to which we belong. We are taught to obey our denomination (or movement) and never to challenge what it teaches." "If the truth be told, we Christians never seem to ask why we do what we do. Instead, we blithely carry out our religious traditions, never asking where they came from." And, one more. "Strikingly, contemporary church thought and practice have been influenced far more by post-Biblical historical events than by NT [New Testament] imperatives and examples. Yet most Christians are unconscious of this influence. Nor are they aware that it has created a slew of cherished, calcified, humanly-devised traditions— all of which are routinely passed off to us as 'Christian.'"[16]

The author limits his coverage to modern church practices, but his questions are just as applicable to many commonly taught and believed doctrines. Most of us have never questioned what we are taught, let alone search for the answers. In this chapter we will look at how we can approach the study of some of these issues, especially when we find no Bible verses or passages that appear to give us clear teaching.

For our first example, I'd like to pose a question that many Christians have never asked. Why do many of us gather for our weekly services in a building that is topped by a steeple? Exactly what is a steeple, what is it for, and where did it originate? We have our questions, so how should we begin our search?

If we do a search for "steeples" in our Bible program it will tell us that zero verses are found. We know that if the Bible has any information on them they are called by another name. Perhaps a beginning point for a search of this nature would be with the Webster's dictionary. It will at least give us a working definition of the word. Here is what my *Webster's New World Dictionary* has under the listing for steeple. "A tower rising above the main structure of a building, esp. of a church, usually capped with a spire."[17] Next question, what is a spire? Most of us don't use that word all that frequently. Turning back a few pages will get us to the listing for spire. At least three separate definitions are given. The second and third seem most pertinent to our inquiry. "2.) The top part of a pointed, tapering object or structure, as a mountain peak, 3.) anything that tapers to a point, as a pointed structure capping a tower or steeple."

So we know that what we see and envision as a steeple is a tower that sits on top of the church building and tapers to a point. We continue to ask, "Why?" "Where did the idea come from?" "What is the origin?"

At this point most of us would ask Google, we'd turn to the internet. Our search phrase of "the origin of the steeple" will yield numerous results. We can get information overload pretty easily. Doubtful that any of us would want to check every one of the possible websites or articles listed. We can be selective. Some will be from encyclopedias and online dictionaries. Perhaps we might begin with those. Quite a few on this topic will be written by others who have had the same questions we have advanced and have done their research. Even though some aren't as good about referencing their sources as we might like we will begin to find that most will give us the same basic information.

Here is information taken from just some of the many articles. The first one was written by Kochava R. Greene, titled *What is the Origin of Church Steeples?* The material is basically the same as you will find on many of the sites. You can do this search for yourself and verify what I'm presenting.

"Steeples, the pointed roofs of churches, have been included in church buildings since the conversion of Constantine and his proclamation making Christianity the official religion of his state. The origins of steeples, however, have been traced back to several different traditions."[18]

Dropping down in this article the author quotes from acclaimed author Joseph Campbell. He is the author of *The Hero with a Thousand Faces* and *Myths to Live By*. The following is quoted from Mr. Campbell.

There are still in existence today remarkable specimens of original phallic symbols, steeples on the churches and obelisks all show the influence of our phallus-worshipping ancestors, including ancient Israelite and Canaanite tribes. These tribes had rituals including the baking of long loaves of bread for blessing, which were, in turn, placed under poles representing the fertility and power of the gods. Eventually, the tall poles became focal points for community worship and were included in the earliest churches as Christianity swept through the region.[19]

Justin Taylor, in his article *History of the Church Steeple* says,

Church steeples can be traced back thousands of years to Egypt and pagan worship. Roman Emperor Constantine and his "Edict of Milan" in 313 C.E. made the Empire officially neutral with regards to religion. Paganism and Christianity could be practiced freely. The stage was set for the melding of ancient pagan architecture (which was widespread in Rome in the form of obelisks which they adopted from Egypt) and earlyChristian architecture. Augustus after defeating Antony and Cleopatra, conquered Egypt in 30 BC. He brought the obelisks dedicated to the Pharaohs Rameses II and Psammetichus II from Heliopolis to Rome.

The phallus played a role in the cult of Osiris in the ancient Egyptian religion. It is widely understood that the obelisk is a phallic symbol honoring and celebrating regeneration of the sun god Ra (Egypt's greatest deity). The obelisk was the first point sun rays hit as it ascended, which the pagans believed symbolized re-birth between earth and heaven.

The Ancient Romans were strongly influenced by the obelisk. There are now more than twice as many obelisks standing in Rome as remain in Egypt. It takes little imagination to see the parallel between the obelisk and the common church steeple, which many historians have pointed out.[20]

Okay, steeples don't seem to be something that would glorify God, do they? But, does the Bible possibly have anything to say about such items? How would we find out? Perhaps you might come across an article or two that points us to some scriptural information.

It is interesting to note that the King James Version of the Bible translates the Hebrew term Asherah as groves, Strong's H842. BDB says of this word, "*Ashera(h)* = groves (for idol worship)" The first definition given says "A Babylonian (Astarte)—Canaanite goddess (of fortune and happiness), the supposed consort of Baal, her images." Another definition given was "sacred trees or poles set up near an altar." *Asherah* is found in the Hebrew Scriptures forty times.

The Companion Bible, Appendix 42, defines asherah. Dr. Bullinger states that it was an upright pillar "connected with Baal-worship" He states that it was associated with the goddess Ashtoreth, "being the representation of the productive (or passive) principal of life, and Baal being the representative of the generative (or active) principle." He continues in the next paragraph, "The image, which represents the Phoenician Ashtoreth of Paphos, as the sole object of worship in her temple, was an upright block of stone, anointed with oil, and covered with an embroidered cloth."[21]

At this point there is a lot of side studies that one could do. As an example, we saw that Dr. Bullinger stated that the pillar was connected with "Baal worship." If we were to do a search for "image of Baal" we would locate two passages in the Old Testament, where this phrase is used, 2 Kings 3:2 and 2 Kings 10:27. We find a different Hebrew word from what we were looking at above. The word is *matstsebah*, Strong's number H4676. The definition given is "something stationed, that is, a *column* or (memorial stone): by analogy an idol—garrison, (standing) image, pillar."

In 2 Kings 10:25–27 where the King James Version says "images of Baal" the Amplified Version says, "As soon as he had finished offering the burnt offering, Jehu said to the guards and to the officers, Go in and slay them; let none escape. And they smote them with the sword; and the guards or runners [before the king] and the officers threw their bodies out and went into the inner dwelling of the house of Baal. They brought out the pillars or obelisks of the house of Baal and burned them" The word is translated as "pillars and obelisks."

If we search the word "image" and do a bit of checking we will find that it is used in Deuteronomy 16:22. In the King James Version we read, "Neither shalt thou set up any image; which the LORD thy God hateth." Numerous other translations make this a bit clearer. Here are what just a few others render this verse. English Standard Version "And you shall not set up a pillar, which the LORD your God hates." The Good News Bible "And do not set up any stone pillar for idol worship; the LORD hates them." The International Standard Version "Furthermore, you are not to erect for yourselves a sacred stone pillar, because the LORD your God detests these things." And, one more, the Jewish Publication Society "Neither shalt thou set thee up a pillar, which the LORD thy God hateth."

In doing this exercise we have uncovered some very interesting information. What we each do with it, how we let it affect us, is outside the scope of this book. But I believe we may have glimpsed just a wee bit where searching for answers to questions can lead us. We won't go through any more exercises here as I believe you get the picture how to do such searches, but maybe we can at least toss out some questions that we could be asking, even about some of the most "sacred" of our Christian teachings.

Let us think about Holy Week and Easter. Have we ever tried to count three days and three nights (the only sign Jesus gave, Matt. 12:40) from Friday to Sunday morning? What do eggs and rabbits have to do with Jesus' death and resurrection?

And, maybe Christmas. Why was December 25th selected as the date to commemorate Jesus' birth? Why do people exchange gifts when the scriptural story of the birth shows the wise men giving gifts to Jesus, not exchanging them among themselves? What do evergreen trees have to do with celebrating the birth of the Messiah? Oh, there are a lot more questions you could ask but this gives you a few to think about. And, these may be enough to keep you busy for a while!

CHAPTER ELEVEN

A BIBLICAL DETECTIVE

I'm sure that you are excited about what you have been reading and learning. I know that it gives me a great deal of excitement to be sharing the techniques of searching and seeking answers with you. Various "cases" have been examined. You have learned how to successfully solve mysteries. No longer are you just a "beat cop" but have now achieved the rank of detective, "Biblical Division."

Okay. We are being a bit theatrical and calling you a biblical detective, but I believe that truly you can be described in that manner. Let me share with you some of the things that qualifies one as a detective. These are all qualities outlined in several internet sources.

A detective must have logic skills and an understanding of alternative solutions to be successful. You have followed the "logical" steps outlined throughout this book and have learned how to look at and consider the numerous and various possibilities in understanding.

Detectives tend to be investigative individuals. You were sincere and serious in desiring to learn how to investigate and search for answers or you would never have purchased this book and continued reading.

Here are some qualities that describe a good detective. They are intellectual, introspective, and inquisitive. They are curious, methodical, rational, analytical, and logical. Many will be enterprising, meaning they're adventurous, ambitious, assertive, extroverted, energetic, confident, and optimistic. Can most of these be applied to you?

A detective makes it his or her job to find the hard-to-get information, one who investigates mysteries of all kinds. It is his or her driving goal and job to discover the truth of a matter. Clearly he or she is an investigator, collecting information in many different ways to solve the mystery and obtain answers to the questions generated along the way.

A detective seeking to solve a crime tries to not overlook any clues. As a biblical detective, we also have to be diligent to look for and collect all the clues along the way. Some may be small and subtle. Asking questions, interviewing victims, witnesses, and "people of interest" is necessary to resolve the "case." As we have repeated over and over in previous chapters, we must continue to ask questions and to seek more input as we proceed.

A good investigator doesn't jump to conclusions—so we can't afford to let of our preconceived ideas and premises lead us into making assumptions and drawing a conclusion before we have completed our investigation. Although there is always a desire to solve the case as quickly as possible a good detective knows that he or she must be extremely thorough, all the T's have got to be crossed and all the I's must be dotted. Our "cases" need to be dealt with in the same manner.

Taking notes as we proceed is very important. Generally the detective will make written notes or dictate notes into his phone. Later those notes will be put into a bit more expanded version while they are still fresh in mind. We will do well to follow that pattern in our searching. As notes accumulate they need to be organized in a logical manner. We may discover that we still have gaps in our investigation and that more questions are generated. We may need to do more "interviews," and look at more Scriptures that may relate to our investigation.

A crime detective may discover that he or she is headed down a wrong road or is engaging in the wrong line of questioning. Hey, that is okay if we find ourselves doing the same type of thing. We merely realign and get back on track. We are still accumulating data. We are adding to our notes. We should be reviewing our notes as we go along. Are there hidden clues there? Do they generate some important questions that haven't previously come to our minds? Do we need to "re-interview" one or more of our "witnesses"?

Investigators, known as detectives, don't work alone. Generally they are supervised by a Lieutenant that is working with a number of investigators, each most likely working on their own assigned case or a self-generated investigation. We as biblical detectives don't work alone. Our Lieutenant is the Holy Spirit. He guides us and helps us realign when we head down the wrong road. We need to continually seek His direction and oversight as we pursue our search.

In our searching of the Scriptures we will be self-initiating investigations and will be developing intelligence. We are gathering information looking toward the solvability of our "case." We put together all of our research in a logical and as factual a manner as possible. With the oversight of our Lieutenant we can bring the case to a close with enough evidence to "convict."

But what if, after all our research, interviewing all of our "witnesses," and following all of the available clues we can't resolve the "case"? This happens frequently with crime investigators. They want to successfully close every case they work, but sometimes they are not able to wrap it up with positive results. Those investigations become what is known as a "cold case." They don't get a lot of time devoted to them from that point on. Other cases have to take priority, but if new leads are received, the case or cases can be reactivated. If we study and search out a word, a verse, a phrase, a topic, or some other biblical item without coming to a definitive conclusion, we too can "shelve" that study for the present. It has become a "cold case". Revelation doesn't come all at one time. The Holy Spirit leads and reveals, but not always in the time frame we may wish for. Patience is something we are instructed to follow after (1 Tim. 6:11). However, it is surprising how often in the midst of another study, another search, one stumbles across some bit of information, a bit of revelation, that necessitates us re-opening the case, the study we shelved earlier. Adding that new bit of evidence may be enough to get a conviction and bring our case to a successful conclusion.

CHAPTER TWELVE

THIS IS YOUR ASSIGNED "CASE"

I n this final chapter we are going to give you a chance to "solve" your own assigned "case." I'm going to give you a passage of Scripture that has generated numerous questions and also a lot of "answers." I'll even give you some questions for you to attempt to answer. After having your opportunity to work through this and hopefully arrive at the answer, I'll share with you my study. There is no "right and wrong" on how you go about this exercise but make notes as you proceed. Your results can be evaluated later.

The Scripture you are going to look at is 1 Corinthians 11:14. The apostle Paul in writing this letter to the church at Corinth asks a question "Doth not even nature itself teach you, that, if a man have long hair, it is a shame unto him?" You have probably heard a number of individuals express what they believe this means. I urge you to lay aside all those beliefs, your own notions and premises. With your mind open to receive where the Holy Spirit will lead you and asking for His direction, you may begin.

Here are some initial questions for you to consider and begin to plan your investigation. Question 1) Does nature teach us that? Question 2) If nature teaches us that, just how? Question 3) How do we define "long"? Question 4) What is shame?

Your notes:

How did I begin?

_____

_____

_____

What did I find?

_____

_____

_____

Other questions that were generated.

_____

_____

_____

Answers to questions.

_____

_____

_____

_____

Other Scriptures that were checked.

_____

_____

_____

What was my process of analysis?

_____

_____

_____

What is the logical organization of my notes on my findings?

_____

_____

_____

Are there other questions that are coming to mind?

_____

_____

_____

Am I able to begin to come up with any possible answers?

_____

_____

_____

What may or may not be keeping me from arriving at a conclusion?

_____

_____

_____

Is this going to be a "cold case" or do I have an answer?

_____

_____

_____

Do I have answers to my initial questions?

_____

_____

_____

Building on everything I discovered I conclude that Paul meant
the following:

_____

_____

_____

_____

I'll share my study. If you don't agree with my conclusion that is fine. This question is one of interest but if we don't all agree it doesn't make us any less loved by God. There is no condemnation in any way. With that said, here is my study.

Does Nature Teach Us That It Is a Shame for a Man to Have Long Hair?

What did Paul mean when he asked the question, "Doth not even nature itself teach you, that, if a man have long hair, it is a shame unto him?"_ (1 Cor. 11:14). That question has been difficult for many to really understand. How does nature teach us that? Some have stated that in nature we often find that the male is the brightly colored one, the one with the longest feathers or hair. The male lion, for example, has the long shaggy mane while the female has no mane at all.

Let us try to understand. We won't go into a long study of this entire passage, which has been misunderstood by many, but will look briefly at the context here and look at the word "nature" as it is used here.

Let us begin our study in verse 4, "Every man praying or prophesying, having his head covered, dishonoureth his head."

The word covered here in verse 4 is literally having (something) down the head. (*Vine's Expository Dictionary of Biblical Words*) Most of the many studies that I looked at on the internet

121

made the assumption that this is speaking of a veil, a piece of cloth. Taking this verse by itself we could not know. However, in all Bible study one needs to look at the context. Jumping ahead to verse 14 we see that Paul is speaking about long hair.

Why would Paul use the word covered and not long hair? Actually, he is saying the same thing. What most of us don't recognize is that Paul, trained in the Torah and in Hebrew, is using a common form of Hebrew poetry called parallelism. *The Angus-Green Bible Handbook* says that the writings of the prophets are for the most part in poetical form. It is further stated that the leading characteristics of Hebrew poetry "may be described generally as consisting in the ornate and elevated character of the style, in the use of certain words and forms of words, in the sententious manner of expression, and especially in what is entitled parallelism;" There are a number of different varieties of parallelism. What we see here is where the "second member is an echo of the first, expressing nearly the same sentiment in a varied form." An example given in the *Angus-Green Bible Handbook* is that of Psalm 19:1. "The heavens declare the glory of God;" being the first member. The second, which echos the first, is "And the firmament showeth His handywork." It is further pointed out that "parallelism often affords important aid in interpretation, by exhibiting the salient points of the passage in their true relation. It is especially useful where the construction is complicated or elliptical, or where uncommon words occur; one member of a sentence which is clear assisting to determine the meaning of another which is ambiguous. Very greatly, too, does this rhythmic

122

arrangement of the thought enhance its force and beauty."[22] Paul uses the word covered in this verse and the next several verses. The meaning is enhanced by the clear statements about long hair in verses 14 and 15.

In this study we won't take the time to look at the following verses but will jump right on down to verses 14 and 15. Just let me state, and you can check it yourself, Paul talks about the creation of man and woman.

Now we come to verse14 that we quoted at the very beginning of this study "Doth not even nature itself teach you, that, if a man have long hair, it is a shame unto him?"

Paul makes a plea to nature, stating something like this: "Look around, you can see it in nature; men have short hair and women have long hair." Notice the word "nature." The Greek word is *phusis*, Strong's G5449. Let us look at some of the definitions as given in *Thayer's Greek Lexicon:* "the nature of things, the force, laws, order of nature." It continues, "as opposed to what is monstrous, abnormal, perverse:" and "birth, physical origin."

Phusis is used in about a dozen places in the New Testament with the same meanings as given by Thayer's. Let us look at one passage, Romans 1:26–27. When men and women participated in homosexual relationships, Paul states that such relationships are "against nature [*phusis*]." It is against the original intent and design for man and woman. God's design for plants, animals, and humans were to maintain their nature and reproduce after their kind. Man and woman were distinct by nature in sex and hair.

The uniqueness of hair length, I believe, was given originally by the Creator with the angels looking over His shoulder. Angels recognize the importance of nature as it relates to the purpose in God's design, that what He created was good. When angels recognize a woman without a covering (long hair) they recognize something out of order (nature) or creation (God's original design). Men and women have basically maintained their hair in accordance to God's creation (nature) much even till this day. Men with exceptionally long hair are given a second look, just as much as a woman with extremely short hair.

In Genesis 1:26–28 we read of the creation of the man and the woman. I'm almost certain that the woman was not given a veil at creation. I think Paul is telling us that she had long hair from the beginning; even "nature" indicates that. Clearly nature teaches that long hair for the man "is a dishonor to him" and long hair for the woman "is a glory to her." (Note again 1 Corinthians 11:15, "But if a woman have long hair, it is a glory to her: for her hair is given her for a covering.")

Paul isn't stating that we need to look at the lions and the various other animals around us, but was just stating that the "very order of nature," "the normal," the way God created and set things should teach us that for a man to let his hair grow long is shameful, that he dishonors his head. I believe that it is interesting to read Revelation 9:7–8. John is relating the vision he had seen and speaking of locusts (just what they may be I'm not pre-pared to say) but in verse 8 he tells us "they had hair as the hair of women." *Jamieson, Fausset and Brown Commentary* says, "long and flowing." Some translations say "long hair." I believe this is a verification of the "normal" state, the "natural order." Women are to have long hair, men shorter hair.

Just checking. Did you possibly proceed with your study in much the same way I did? As I said, there is no "right or wrong" way. Were our answers close? Did I look at some things you didn't even think of or didn't occur to you? Would you or possi-bly, will you, go back through this little exercise and take a bit different approach?

Before concluding, I have one or two other important things to pass along to you. I was taught when I was first beginning to study the Bible that if I wanted to study a subject I should search out every verse in the Bible on that subject and then try to use all of them to come to an understanding. The idea sounded good and I tried to follow it, but often, found passages that seemed to contradict one another and led to confusion. A few years ago I was given the truth on this. Although the Bible is inspired by God and is "profitable for doctrine, for reproof, for correction, for instruction in righteousness" (2 Tim. 3:16), it wasn't all writ-ten directly to you and me. God spoke or gave instruction to dif-ferent people at different times through the various covenants. What He spoke to the Israelites at Mount Sinai is good and holy words, but they weren't spoken to you and me. We have been given a new covenant. This entails more study, but keep in mind who the Scripture may have been intended for, and ask if it still applies to you and me. Many still do!

I mentioned this back in chapter 3 but feel that it would be good to repeat it as we conclude. It has been my experience that when the Spirit leads us into truth, when we are given revelation, we can become very judgmental of others who may still be in their ignorance. We may begin to compare ourselves among ourselves, which Paul tells us is unwise (1 Cor. 10:12), and somehow begin to feel that we are somehow superior to or in some way better than others. Paul tells us in Romans 14 that we should not be judging another if they believe and do things differently. He says, "Who art thou that judgest another man's servant?" (Rom. 14:4). Our view of others should be just as God's view. We need to "wink at" and overlook any ignorance that may be there and concentrate on truly repenting and changing our own thinking. Of course, we may be praying for others to receive the revelation we have received but must keep in mind that it is in His "due season" and leave it in His hands.

Well, we have come to end of our time together in this book. Have we covered everything there is to know about searching the Scriptures? No! Not by any means, but you have been given a solid foundation and framework to build upon. You have much more to work with than I did when I first started searching many years ago.

Thank you for reading my book. I truly and sincerely hope I have been a help and a blessing to you.

ABOUT THE AUTHOR

G arry D. Pifer has been a reader and student of the Bible for over sixty years. For the last twenty-five plus years he has been learning and practicing the steps and keys outlined in this book, searching out the hidden treasures in God's Word. Some of his personal studies have been published in an independent journal and many have been posted to the internet. Garry and his wife of over fifty-five years are the parents of four grown children and currently reside in South-Central Kentucky.

Garry may be contacted by E-mail: garrydpifer@gmail.com

NOTES

1 J. I. Packer, *Fundamentalism and the Word of God: Some Evangelical Principles* (Grand Rapids, MI: William B. Eerdmans Publishing Co.), pp 69–70.

2 Adam Clarke, author; Ralph Earle, editor, *Adam Clarke's Commentary on the Bible*, Beacon Hill Press of Kansas City, Kansas City, MO © 1967 (originally published 1810)

3 John Gill, *Exposition of the Bible* (Kindle edition) © 2019 Patristic Publishing, Woolworth Ave., Omaha, NE. This material is available in the public domain.

4 A. T. Robertson, *Word Pictures in the New Testament* in 6 volumes. Vol. 1, 2, 3, 4, in public domain. Vol. 5 © 1932, renewal 1960 Broadman Press, expired Dec. 31, 2006. Free non-commercial distribution. Vol. 6 © 1933, renewal 1960 Broadman Press, expired Dec. 31, 2007. Free non-commercial distribution.

5 John Gill, *Exposition of the Bible* (Kindle edition) © 2019 Patristic Publishing, Woolworth Ave., Omaha, NE. This material is available in the public domain.

[6] John D. Davis, *Davis Dictionary of the Bible, Fourth Revised Edition*, © 1898, 1903, 1911, 1924 by the Trustees of the Presbyterian Board of Publication and Sabbath-School Work. Reprinted by Baker Book House under special arrangement with the Board of Christian Education of the Presbyterian Church in the United States of America. Twenty-first printing, July 1973.

[7] *What is Death? www.truthaboutdeath.com/blog/id/1585/what-is-death*

[8] *Death & Dying What is Death* www.death-and-dying.org/what-is-death.htm/

[9] Christopher A. Pallis, *Encyclopedia Britannica Death www.britannica.com/science/death*

. *BusinessDictionary death* www.businessdictionary.com/definition/death.html

[10] *BusinessDictionary death* www.businessdictionary.com/definition/death.html

[11] *DADABHAGWAN.org* https://www.dadabhagwan.org/path-to-happiness/spiritual-science/science-of-death/what-is-death/

[12] *Compellingtruth Death – What Does the Bible Say About It?* www.compellingtruth.org/bible-death.html

[13] Dr. Paul M. Elliott, *What is the Biblical Definition of Death?* http://ttw2.org/articles_pdf/tq0374.pdf

[14] Dr. E. W. Bullinger, *The Companion Bible,* dates 1906–1922, Kregel Publications, available at ewbullingerbooks.com

[15] Rabbi Michael L. Rodkinson, *The History of the Talmud* (divided into two volumes) © 1903, New Talmud Publishing Co., 1117 Simpson St., New York City, NY, Vol. II pg. 70

[16] Frank Viola, *PAGAN CHRISTIANITY: The Origins of Our Modern Church Practices,* © 2002 by Present Testimony Ministry, ptmin@aol.com / www.ptmin.org

[17] *Third College Edition* **Webster's New World Dictionary**® of *American English,* © 1994 by Simon & Schuster, Inc., A Paramount Communications Company.

[18] Kochina R. Green, *What Is the Origin of Church Steeples,* http://classroom.synonym.com/what-is-the-orogin-of-church-steeples-12078900.htm

[19] . Joseph Campbell, author of *The Hero With a Thousand Faces* © 1949, published by Pantheon Books and *Myths to Live By* © 1972, published by Viking

[20] Justin Taylor, *History of the Church Steeple,*
http://werdsmith.com/genesology/OR2AbZFhY

[21] Dr. E. W. Bullinger, *The Companion Bible,* dates 1906–1922, Kregel Publications, available at ewbullingerbooks.com

[22] Joseph Angus, M. A., D. D., thoroughly revised and in part re-written by Samuel G. Green, D. D., *The Bible Handbook,* the reprint of the revised edition 1952, third impression 1961, Fleming H. Revell Company, Westwood, NJ. Pages 558–562